The Scarlet Letter

A Haunting Tale of Sin, Shame & Redemption in a Strict Puritan Society

A Modern Translation

Adapted for the Contemporary Reader

Nathaniel Hawthorne

Translated by Tim Zengerink

Table of Contents

Preface
Message to the Reader

Rebuilding the Greatest Library in Human History

Thousands of years ago, the Library of Alexandria was the heart of global knowledge — a sanctuary where the wisdom of every known civilization was gathered and shared freely.

And then, it was lost.

Now, we're rebuilding it — and you are invited to join us.

At the Library of Alexandria, we've set out to make every book available to every person on Earth — not just in print, but in every language, every format, and for every reader.

Here's how we do it:

- **Deluxe Print Editions at True Printing Cost** - Order any book as a high-quality paperback, elegant hardcover, or stunning boxset — and only pay what it costs to print. No markups. No middlemen.
- **Unlimited Access to the Greatest Works** - Enjoy thousands of timeless classics — from Plato to Shakespeare to Tolstoy — in beautiful, modern eBook and audiobook editions. Read and listen without limits — for every reader, everywhere.
- **Modern Translations for Every Language & Dialect** - We're reimagining the classics in clear, accessible language — and translating them into every dialect imaginable. Everyone deserves to understand humanity's greatest ideas.

When you visit **LibraryofAlexandria.com**, you're not just accessing books — you're joining a global movement to restore, preserve, and share the wisdom of civilization.

Join us today at LibraryofAlexandria.com

Together, we'll ensure the light of human wisdom never fades again.

With gratitude,

The Modern Library of Alexandria Team

Visit:
www.libraryofalexandria.com
Or scan the code below:

Introduction to The Scarlet Letter

A Portrait of Human Struggle Beneath the Cloak of Puritanism

Nathaniel Hawthorne's *The Scarlet Letter*, first published in 1850, stands as a cornerstone of American literature—an enduring exploration of sin, guilt, identity, and redemption set against the bleak backdrop of 17th-century Puritan New England. More than just a historical novel, it is a psychological and philosophical meditation on the nature of human fallibility, societal judgment, and the complex interplay between inner truth and public perception. With its evocative symbolism, moral nuance, and haunting atmosphere, *The Scarlet Letter* has remained an essential work for generations of readers, critics, and scholars.

Set in a stern and pious Massachusetts Bay Colony, the novel tells the story of Hester Prynne, a woman condemned by her community after bearing an illegitimate child. Forced to wear a scarlet "A" for adultery upon her chest, Hester becomes both a target of scorn and a figure of fascination. But rather than being crushed by her punishment, she transforms into a symbol of strength, compassion, and quiet defiance. Her story is one of endurance, dignity, and evolution—contrasted sharply with those around her, whose secrets fester beneath the veneer of righteousness.

At its heart, *The Scarlet Letter* is not just about Hester's transgression, but about the hypocrisy of a society that punishes women for passion while silently protecting men from consequence. It is about the corrosive effects of hidden guilt, the complexity of forgiveness, and the long road to moral clarity. Through his intricate characters—Hester, Reverend Arthur

Dimmesdale, Roger Chillingworth, and young Pearl—Hawthorne crafts a parable that challenges simplistic definitions of good and evil, and invites readers to look beyond social labels to the deeper currents of the human soul.

Hawthorne, a descendent of Puritan settlers and a critic of their legacy, uses this novel to wrestle with the moral rigidity and spiritual repression of America's early settlers. But he does so with empathy and psychological depth, making *The Scarlet Letter* not just a historical critique but a timeless examination of the burdens we carry and the ways we seek release. His prose is rich, symbolic, and deliberate, drawing the reader into a world of shadows and revelations where redemption is always just out of reach—but never wholly lost.

Sin, Secrecy, and the Search for Redemption

The Scarlet Letter centers on four principal characters, each representing a different moral struggle and response to sin. Hester Prynne, the novel's courageous heroine, stands apart from the society that condemns her. Although marked and humiliated by the community, she neither protests her punishment nor reveals the name of her lover. Her strength lies in her ability to accept the consequences of her actions and to live with integrity in the face of scorn. Over time, the scarlet letter—originally a symbol of shame—becomes a badge of honor, reflecting her quiet acts of charity, resilience, and wisdom.

Reverend Arthur Dimmesdale, in contrast, is consumed by internal torment. As the secret father of Hester's child, he hides behind his clerical position while suffering the psychological toll of concealed guilt. His physical and emotional decline reflects the destructive power of hypocrisy and the consequences of failing to acknowledge one's truth. While Hester bears her shame openly and grows from it, Dimmesdale withers under the weight of secrecy, illustrating the stark difference between outward punishment and inner torment.

Roger Chillingworth, Hester's estranged husband, embodies a different kind of sin: the cold, calculated desire for revenge. Masquerading as a physician, he attaches himself to Dimmesdale under the pretense of healing, all the while slowly destroying the minister's body and spirit. Chillingworth's obsession with vengeance turns him into something less than human—a figure of malice and moral decay. His story warns of the spiritual cost of unforgiveness and the consuming nature of hatred.

Then there is Pearl, Hester's daughter, a living embodiment of her mother's sin but also of her vitality and independence. Pearl is wild, intuitive, and untamed—a symbol of natural truth in contrast to the artificial codes of Puritan society. She forces those around her to confront their lies and inconsistencies. Through Pearl, Hawthorne injects a thread of hope, suggesting that something pure and true can emerge from even the most condemned beginnings.

Each of these characters represents a different moral trajectory: Hester's redemptive transformation, Dimmesdale's inward collapse, Chillingworth's descent into monstrosity, and Pearl's potential for a freer future. Hawthorne is less interested in assigning blame than in exploring how different people live with—and are changed by—their moral failures.

The Puritan setting is essential to this exploration. It is a society governed by strict theocratic laws, where sin is publicly punished and individual will is subsumed by communal control. But Hawthorne, writing in the 19th century, infuses this historical portrait with a Romantic and psychological sensibility. He sees beyond the black-and-white morality of his forebears, recognizing that truth and virtue are far more nuanced and complex than the Puritan order allows. In doing so, he exposes the limitations of legalistic morality and underscores the necessity of compassion and personal conscience.

The Scarlet Letter is also a novel of immense symbolic richness. The scarlet "A," Pearl's presence, the forest, the scaffold, and even the light and shadows that dance through the story—all carry layered meanings. The forest, for instance, serves as a space of wildness and possibility, where characters can escape the strictures of society and encounter a more honest version of themselves. The scaffold is a site of shame and confession, where public and private truths collide. Hawthorne's use of symbol and setting deepens the psychological drama, turning external events into expressions of internal transformation.

Hawthorne's Legacy and the Novel's Enduring Power

Nathaniel Hawthorne's *The Scarlet Letter* occupies a unique place in American literature. It was one of the first American novels to gain critical acclaim both domestically and abroad, and it helped establish the literary seriousness of American fiction at a time when the young nation was still developing its cultural identity. Hawthorne's blend of psychological depth, moral inquiry, and historical context created a model for the American novel that would influence countless writers—from Herman Melville and Henry James to Toni Morrison and Margaret Atwood.

The novel's central themes—shame, identity, social judgment, and redemption—remain powerfully relevant in modern times. In an age of public shaming, viral condemnation, and intense scrutiny of private behavior, Hawthorne's exploration of how societies treat moral transgression is more timely than ever. His novel invites us to ask: Who has the right to judge? What is the path to forgiveness? Can a person redefine themselves in the eyes of a world that refuses to forget?

Moreover, *The Scarlet Letter* is a profound meditation on the role of women in society. Hester Prynne's quiet defiance, her ability to survive and even thrive within a system designed to break her, makes her one of the earliest feminist figures in American literature. She raises her child alone, makes a living through her own skill, and maintains a sense of self-worth despite relentless condemnation. Hawthorne does not make her into a martyr or a saint, but a human being—flawed, proud, enduring.

Modern readers continue to find new meanings in Hawthorne's tale. For some, it is a story about moral complexity in a world hungry for simple answers. For others, it is a critique of religious extremism and the dangers of confusing law with virtue. For still others, it is a deeply human story about the need to be seen, known, and forgiven. Its richness lies in its ability to speak to all of these dimensions at once—and to leave space for reflection long after the final page is turned.

Hawthorne himself understood that sin is not something that can be washed away by punishment or erased by conformity. It is something that must be understood, carried, and transformed. *The Scarlet Letter* does not end in total tragedy nor in triumph, but in a quiet recognition of life's ambiguity. It offers no easy resolutions, only the hope that in the face of suffering, truth and love may still prevail.

As you enter the shadowed world of Puritan Boston, be prepared to encounter more than a tale of historical shame. This is a novel that looks unflinchingly at the depths of the human heart—its desires, its failings, its strength. It reminds us that behind every label, there is a person. Behind every sin, a story. And that, perhaps, is the greatest message of *The Scarlet Letter*: that grace is not something given by society, but something found within.

The Custom-House

Vignette—Wild Rose

The Scarlet Letter.

Chapter 1: The Prison Door.

A crowd of bearded men wearing somber-colored clothing and gray, tall pointed hats mixed with women, some with hoods covering their heads and others with their heads uncovered, had gathered in front of a wooden building whose door was constructed with heavy oak timber and decorated with iron spikes.

The Founders of any new colony, no matter what ideal vision of human goodness and happiness they might have originally planned, have always recognized among their first practical needs the necessity of setting aside a portion of the untouched land as a cemetery, and another portion as the location for a prison. Following this pattern, we can safely assume that Boston's founding fathers had constructed the first jailhouse somewhere near Cornhill, almost as quickly as they had designated the first burial ground on Isaac Johnson's property, around his grave, which later became the center of all the gathered tombs in King's Chapel's old churchyard. What is certain is that some fifteen or twenty years after the town's establishment, the wooden jail already showed weather stains and other signs of aging, which gave an even darker appearance to its heavy-browed and somber facade. The rust on the massive ironwork of its oak door appeared more ancient than anything else in the New World. Like everything connected to crime, it seemed never to have experienced a time of youth. In front of this ugly building, between it and the wheel tracks of the street, lay a patch of grass, heavily overgrown with burdock, pigweed, apple-peru, and other unsightly plants, which clearly found something suitable in the soil that had so early produced the dark flower of civilized society—a prison. But on one side of the entrance, rooted almost at the doorstep, stood a wild rosebush, covered in this month of June with its delicate blossoms, which one might imagine offered their fragrance and fragile beauty to the prisoner as he entered, and to the condemned criminal as he emerged to face his fate, as a sign that Nature's deep heart could feel compassion and show kindness to him.

This rose bush, through an unusual twist of fate, has survived throughout history; but whether it simply endured from the harsh ancient wilderness, long after the massive pines and oaks that once shaded it had fallen,—or whether, as reliable sources suggest, it grew beneath the feet of the blessed Ann Hutchinson as she walked through the prison door,—we will not attempt to decide. Discovering it positioned so clearly at the beginning of our story, which is about to emerge from that unlucky entrance, we could hardly avoid picking one of its blossoms and offering it to the reader. It may serve, we hope, to represent some gentle moral flower that might be discovered along the way, or provide relief from the grim ending of a story about human weakness and grief.

Chapter 2: The Marketplace.

The grassy area in front of the jail on Prison Lane was filled with a large crowd of Boston residents on a summer morning more than two hundred years ago, all staring intently at the heavy iron-reinforced oak door. Among any other group of people, or during a later time in New England's history, the harsh sternness that hardened the bearded faces of these citizens would have suggested some terrible event was about to take place. It could have meant nothing less than the expected execution of some notorious criminal, whose death sentence from a legal court had simply confirmed what the public already believed. However, given the early strict nature of Puritan society, such a conclusion couldn't be drawn with complete certainty. It's possible that a lazy indentured servant, or a disobedient child whose parents had turned over to the authorities, was about to be punished at the whipping post. Perhaps a religious dissenter—an Antinomian, a Quaker, or some other nonconformist—was going to be whipped and driven from the town, or maybe a lazy, wandering Native American, made unruly by the white settlers' alcohol, was about to be beaten and forced back into the forest. It could also be that a witch, like old Mistress Hibbins, the bitter-natured widow of a magistrate, was going to be hanged on the gallows. In any of these situations, the onlookers displayed the same serious behavior, which was fitting for a community where religion and law were nearly the same thing, and where both were so deeply woven into people's character that the gentlest and harshest forms of public punishment were equally treated with reverence and fear. A lawbreaker could expect very little compassion from such observers at the place of execution. On the flip side, a punishment that in our time would bring mockery and shame might back then have carried almost the same grave dignity as a death sentence.

It was worth noting on that summer morning when our story begins that the women in the crowd—and there were several of them—seemed particularly interested in whatever punishment was about to take place. The era lacked the refinement that would have prevented women in their petticoats and farthingales from venturing into public spaces and pushing their substantial figures into the crowd closest to the execution scaffold when the occasion called for it. Both morally and physically, those wives and young women of old English heritage possessed a coarser nature than their beautiful descendants who came six or seven generations later. Throughout that ancestral line, each successive mother passed down to her child a fainter glow, more delicate and fleeting beauty, and a frailer physical build, if not a character with less strength and substance than her own. The women now gathered around the prison door lived less than fifty years after the time when the masculine Elizabeth had served as a fitting representative of their gender. They were her fellow countrywomen, and the beef and ale of their homeland, along with moral nourishment that was equally unrefined, formed a large part of their makeup. The bright morning sun therefore illuminated broad shoulders and full chests, and round, rosy cheeks that had matured on that distant island and had barely grown pale or thin in New England's climate. Furthermore, these women—most of whom appeared to be married—spoke with a boldness and fullness that would shock us today, both in terms of what they said and how loudly they said it.

"Ladies," said a stern-faced woman of fifty, "I'll share my thoughts with you. It would greatly benefit the public if we women, being mature in age and church members with good standing, were given authority over such female wrongdoers as this Hester Prynne. What do you think, friends? If that shameless woman had stood trial before the five of us gathered here together, would she have received such a lenient sentence as the honorable magistrates have given her? Indeed, I think not!"

"People are saying," another person remarked, "that Reverend Master Dimmesdale, her devout pastor, is deeply troubled that such a disgraceful situation has affected his congregation."

"The magistrates are God-fearing gentlemen, but they're far too merciful—that's the truth," added a third elderly woman. "At the very least, they should have branded Hester Prynne's forehead with a hot iron. Madam Hester would have flinched at that, I guarantee you. But she—the shameless woman—won't care much about what they put on the front of her dress! Why, look, she can cover it with a brooch or some other ungodly decoration, and walk the streets as boldly as ever!"

"Ah, but," interrupted a young wife more gently, holding a child by the hand, "no matter how she tries to hide the mark, the pain of it will always remain in her heart."

"What are we doing talking about marks and brands, whether on the front of her dress or carved into her forehead?" shouted another woman, the ugliest and most merciless of these self-appointed judges. "This woman has brought disgrace upon all of us, and she deserves to die. Isn't there a law for this? There certainly is, both in the Bible and in our legal code. So let the officials, who have made that law meaningless, blame themselves when their own wives and daughters lose their way!"

"Have mercy on us, good woman," a man in the crowd called out, "is there no goodness in women except what comes from a healthy fear of being hanged? That's the harshest thing said yet! Quiet now, neighbors! The lock is turning in the prison door, and here comes Mistress Prynne herself."

The jail door burst open from inside, and the first figure to emerge was like a dark shadow stepping into sunlight—the stern and forbidding town beadle, carrying a sword at his side and gripping his official staff. This man embodied in his very appearance the harsh and unforgiving nature of Puritan law, which he was responsible for enforcing in its most direct and personal application to wrongdoers. Extending his official staff with his left hand, he placed his right hand on the shoulder of a young woman, drawing her forward in this manner. However, when they reached the prison doorway, she pushed him away with a gesture that showed both natural dignity and strength of character, then stepped into the open air as though moving by her own choice. She carried in her arms an infant, a baby about three months old, who blinked and turned its tiny face away from the bright daylight, since the child had known only the dim gray light of a prison cell or other dark rooms within the jail during its short life.

When the young woman—the mother of this child—stood

completely exposed before the crowd, her first instinct seemed to be to hold the infant tightly against her chest; not so much from maternal love, but rather to hide a particular symbol that was sewn or attached to her clothing. Within moments, however, wisely realizing that one mark of her disgrace would hardly be enough to conceal another, she lifted the baby onto her arm, and with a face burning red from embarrassment, yet wearing a proud smile and a look that refused to show shame, she gazed around at the people of her town and her neighbors. On the front of her dress, made of fine red fabric and surrounded by intricate embroidery and elaborate decorative patterns of gold thread, was the letter A. It was crafted so skillfully, and with such rich and magnificent creativity, that it appeared to be the perfect final touch to complete the outfit she was wearing; clothing that was splendid enough to match the fashion preferences of that time period, but far more extravagant than what the colony's laws governing luxury and dress permitted.

The young woman was tall, with a figure of perfect elegance on a grand scale. She had dark and thick hair, so shiny that it reflected the sunlight with a brilliant gleam, and a face which, beyond being beautiful from the symmetry of her features and the richness of her skin tone, possessed the commanding presence that comes from a prominent brow and deep black eyes. She was refined, too, in the way that feminine nobility was understood in those times; marked by a certain formality and dignity, rather than by the delicate, fleeting, and indefinable grace that is now recognized as its hallmark. And never had Hester Prynne appeared more refined, in the old-fashioned sense of the word, than when she emerged from the prison. Those who had known her before, and had expected to see her dulled and darkened by a catastrophic shadow, were amazed, and even shocked, to discover how her beauty blazed forth, and created a radiant aura around the misfortune and shame that surrounded her. It may be true that, to a perceptive observer, there was something intensely painful about it. Her clothing, which she had indeed created for this moment while in prison, and had designed largely according to her own imagination, seemed to express her spirit's attitude, the reckless desperation of her state of mind, through its wild and striking uniqueness. But the feature that captured every gaze, and seemed to transform the woman wearing it—so that both men and women who had been closely familiar with Hester Prynne now felt as though they were seeing her for the first time—was that Scarlet Letter, so elaborately embroidered and decorated upon her chest. It had the power of an enchantment, removing her from normal human relationships, and surrounding her in a world of her own.

"She's certainly skilled with her needle," commented one of the women watching; "but has any woman before this shameless hussy ever found such a way to show it off! Why, friends, what is this but laughing in the faces of our godly magistrates, and turning into a source of pride what those worthy gentlemen intended as punishment?"

"It would be good," muttered the most stern-faced of the old women, "if we stripped Madam Hester's fine gown off her delicate shoulders; and as for the red letter, which she has stitched so skillfully, I'll provide a piece of my own rough flannel, to make a more suitable one!"

"Oh, quiet, neighbors, quiet!" whispered their youngest companion; "don't let her hear you! Every single stitch in that embroidered letter has caused her pain in her heart."

The stern official now made a gesture with his staff.

"Make way, good people, make way, in the King's name!" he shouted. "Clear a path; and I promise you, Mrs. Prynne will be placed where every man, woman, and child can get a good look at her fine clothing, from now until an hour past noon. God bless the righteous Colony of Massachusetts, where sin is brought out into the light of day! Come along, Madam Hester, and display your scarlet letter in the marketplace!"

A path was immediately cleared through the crowd of onlookers. Led by the town official, and followed by a disorganized parade of stern-faced men and unfriendly-looking women, Hester Prynne walked toward the location designated for her punishment. A group of excited and curious schoolboys, understanding little about what was happening except that it gave them time off from school, ran ahead of her, constantly turning their heads to gaze at her face, at the blinking baby in her arms, and at the shameful letter on her chest. The distance from the prison door to the marketplace wasn't very far in those times. From the prisoner's perspective, though, it could have been considered quite a long journey; because despite her proud bearing, she perhaps suffered anguish from every step taken by those who crowded to watch her, as though her heart had been thrown into the street for everyone to kick and stomp on. In human nature, however, there exists a feature that is both amazing and compassionate—that someone who suffers never fully grasps the severity of their pain through the immediate torment, but mainly through the lasting ache that festers afterward. With an almost calm manner, therefore, Hester Prynne walked through this part of her trial, and arrived at a kind of platform at the western end of the marketplace. It stood almost directly under the roof edge of Boston's first church, and seemed to be permanently installed there.

In reality, this platform was part of a punishment device that has been nothing more than a historical relic for the past two or three generations, but in earlier times was considered as effective at promoting good citizenship as the guillotine was among the French revolutionaries. It was, simply put, the pillory platform, and above it stood the framework of that disciplinary instrument, designed to lock a person's head in its tight grip and hold it up for everyone to see. The very essence of public shame was captured and made real in this contraption of wood and iron. There can be no greater violation, I believe, against our shared humanity—regardless of what crimes a person may have committed—no violation more outrageous than preventing the guilty person from hiding their face in shame, which was exactly what this punishment was designed to do. In Hester Prynne's case, however, as often happened with others, her sentence required that she stand for a certain period on the platform, but without having to endure the grip around her neck and the head restraint, which was the most cruel feature of this horrible device. Understanding her role well, she climbed a set of wooden steps and was put on display before the gathered crowd, positioned about shoulder-height above the street level.

If there had been a Catholic among the crowd of Puritans, he might have seen in this beautiful woman, so striking in her clothing and bearing, and with the baby at her breast, something that would remind him of the image of Divine Motherhood, which so many famous painters have competed with one another to portray; something that would remind him, indeed, but only by contrast, of that sacred image of pure motherhood, whose child was destined to save the world. Here, there was the stain of the deepest sin in the most sacred aspect of human life, creating such an effect that the world was only darker because of this woman's beauty, and more lost because of the child that she had given birth to.

The scene carried a mixture of awe, the kind that always accompanies witnessing guilt and shame in another person, before society becomes corrupt enough to smile rather than shudder at such displays. Those who witnessed Hester Prynne's disgrace had not yet lost their moral simplicity. They were stern enough to watch her execution, had that been her sentence, without questioning its harshness, but they lacked the callousness of a more degenerate social order that would find only amusement in such a spectacle. Even if anyone had been inclined to mock the situation, such impulses would have been suppressed and overwhelmed by the solemn presence of distinguished men including the Governor and several of his advisors, a judge, a general, and the town's ministers, all of whom sat or stood on the meeting-house balcony, gazing down at the platform. When such important figures could participate in the spectacle without compromising the dignity or respect due to their rank and position, one could safely conclude that this legal punishment carried serious and meaningful weight. Therefore, the crowd remained somber and grave. The unfortunate woman endured her ordeal as best she could under the crushing burden of a thousand merciless eyes, all fixed upon her and focused on her chest. The weight of their stares was almost unbearable. Being impulsive and passionate by nature, she had steeled herself to face the sharp attacks and poisonous strikes of public scorn, expressed through every form of insult imaginable. However, there was something far more terrifying about the crowd's solemn attitude that made her wish instead to see all those stern faces twisted with mocking laughter, with herself as their target. If a burst of laughter had erupted from the crowd—with each man, each woman, each sharp-voiced child adding their own voice to the chorus—Hester Prynne might have answered them all with a bitter and contemptuous smile. But under the oppressive punishment she was destined to bear, she felt at times as though she might scream with all the power in her lungs and throw herself from the scaffold to the ground below, or else lose her mind completely.

Yet there were moments when the entire scene, in which she was the most prominent figure, seemed to disappear from her sight, or at least appeared dimly before her, like a collection of poorly formed and ghostly images. Her mind, and particularly her memory, was unusually active, and kept bringing forth other scenes than this crudely carved street of a small town, on the border of the Western frontier; other faces than those that were scowling at her from beneath the brims of those tall, pointed hats. Memories the most trivial and insignificant, moments of childhood and school days, games, childish arguments, and the small household details of her unmarried years, came flooding back to her, mixed with recollections of whatever was most serious in her later life; one image exactly as clear as another; as if all were of equal significance, or all equally like a performance. Perhaps it was a natural mechanism of her soul, to ease itself, through the display of these dreamlike visions, from the harsh weight and severity of what was real.

Regardless of what might be said, the pillory's platform provided Hester Prynne with a vantage point that revealed the entire path she had walked since her joyful childhood. Standing on that wretched height, she once again saw her home village in Old England and her father's house; a crumbling structure of gray stone that looked impoverished, yet still displayed a faded coat of arms above the entrance, marking its ancient noble heritage. She saw her father's face, with his bare forehead and dignified white beard that cascaded over his old-style Elizabethan collar; she also saw her mother's face, bearing that expression of careful and worried love that she always remembered, and which, even after her mother's death, had often placed the barrier of gentle disapproval in her daughter's way. She saw her own face, radiant with youthful beauty, lighting up the entire surface of the dark mirror where she used to look at herself. There she glimpsed another face, that of an elderly man, a pale, thin, scholarly appearance, with eyes dulled and clouded by the lamplight that had helped him study many heavy books. Yet those same clouded eyes possessed a strange, piercing ability when their owner intended to examine the human spirit. This figure from the study and monastery, as Hester Prynne's feminine imagination clearly remembered, was slightly misshapen, with his left shoulder somewhat higher than his right. Next appeared before her, in memory's collection of images, the complex and narrow streets, the towering gray houses, the massive cathedrals, and the public buildings, old in age and charming in design, of a European city; where a new existence had waited for her, still connected to the deformed scholar; a new existence, but one that sustained itself on ancient elements, like a patch of green moss on a deteriorating wall. Finally, replacing these changing scenes, returned the rough marketplace of the Puritan settlement, with all the townspeople gathered and directing their harsh stares at Hester Prynne—yes, at herself—who stood on the pillory's platform, a baby in her arms, and the letter A, in scarlet, elaborately embroidered with golden thread, upon her chest!

Standing on the Miserable Eminence

Could this really be happening? She held the child against her chest so tightly that it cried out; she looked down at the scarlet letter and even touched it with her finger to convince herself that both the baby and her disgrace were real. Yes! These were the facts of her life—everything else had disappeared!

Chapter 3: The Recognition.

From this overwhelming awareness of being watched so harshly by everyone around her, the woman wearing the scarlet letter finally found relief when she spotted a figure at the edge of the crowd that completely captured her attention. A Native American man stood there dressed in his traditional clothing, but Native Americans visited the English settlements often enough that one of them wouldn't normally have caught Hester Prynne's attention at a time like this, and certainly wouldn't have pushed all other thoughts and sights from her mind. Next to the Native American, clearly keeping him company, stood a white man wearing a bizarre mix of civilized and primitive clothing.

He was short, with a lined face that couldn't quite be called old yet. His features showed remarkable intelligence, like someone who had developed his mind so thoroughly that it couldn't help but shape his physical appearance and show itself through unmistakable signs. Though he had tried to hide or downplay the oddity through what seemed like a careless mix of clothing, it was clear enough to Hester Prynne that one of this man's shoulders was higher than the other. The moment she saw that thin face and the slight deformity of his figure, she pressed her baby to her chest with such violent force that the poor child cried out in pain again. But the mother didn't seem to hear it.

When he arrived at the market-place, and some time before she noticed him, the stranger had fixed his gaze on Hester Prynne. At first, his attention seemed casual, like someone who was mainly used to looking inward, and for whom outside events held little worth or significance, unless they connected to something in his own thoughts. Very quickly, though, his stare became sharp and piercing. A twisting sense of horror swept across his face, like a snake sliding rapidly over it, pausing briefly with all its coiled movements visible to see. His expression grew dark with some intense emotion, which he nonetheless controlled instantly through sheer willpower, so that except for a single moment, his face might have appeared calm. After a short time, the disturbance became almost unnoticeable, and eventually disappeared into the depths of his character. When he discovered that Hester Prynne's eyes were locked on his own, and saw that she seemed to recognize him, he slowly and deliberately raised his finger, made a motion with it in the air, and placed it against his lips.

Then, gently placing his hand on the shoulder of a local resident standing beside him, he spoke to the man in a polite and respectful way.

"Please tell me, good sir," he said, "who is this woman, and why has she been put here for public humiliation?"

"You must be new to this area, friend," the townsman replied, looking with curiosity at the person asking the question and his wild-looking companion, "otherwise you would certainly have heard about Mistress Hester Prynne and her wicked actions. She has caused quite a scandal, I assure you, in the church of the godly Master Dimmesdale."

"You speak the truth," the other man replied. "I am indeed a stranger and have been wandering against my wishes. I have suffered terrible misfortunes both at sea and on land, and was held captive for a long time among the native peoples to the south. This Indian has now brought me here so that I might be freed from my imprisonment. Would you be so kind, then, to tell me about Hester Prynne—do I have her name correct?—about this woman's crimes and what has led her to that platform over there?"

"Really, friend; and I imagine it must bring joy to your heart, after your troubles and time spent in the wilderness," said the townsman, "to find yourself, at last, in a land where wrongdoing is sought out, and punished before the eyes of rulers and people; as here in our godly New England. That woman over there, Sir, you must understand, was the wife of a certain learned man, English by birth, but who had lived for a long time in Amsterdam, from where, some time ago, he decided to cross over and join his fate with us of the Massachusetts. For this purpose, he sent his wife ahead of him, staying behind himself to take care of some necessary business. Indeed, good Sir, in about two years, or less, that the woman has been living here in Boston, no news has come of this learned gentleman, Master Prynne; and his young wife, you see, being left to her own poor judgment—"

"Ah! I see what you mean," said the stranger with a bitter smile. "Such a learned man as you describe should have discovered this in his books as well. And who, if you don't mind me asking, sir, might be the father of that baby—I'd guess it's about three or four months old—that Mistress Prynne is holding in her arms?"

"Truly, friend, that matter remains a mystery; and the Daniel who will explain it is still missing," answered the townsman. "Madam Hester absolutely refuses to speak, and the magistrates have put their heads together in vain. Perhaps the guilty one stands looking on at this sad spectacle, unknown to man, and forgetting that God sees him."

"The scholar," the stranger remarked with another smile, "should come himself to investigate the mystery."

"It would be good for him if he's still alive," the townsman replied. "Now, good sir, our Massachusetts authorities, considering that this woman is young and beautiful, and was undoubtedly strongly tempted into her downfall—and that, furthermore, her husband is most likely dead at sea—they have not dared to enforce the full severity of our righteous law against her. The penalty for her crime is death. But in their great mercy and compassion, they have sentenced Mistress Prynne to stand for only three hours on the pillory platform, and then for the rest of her natural life, to wear a mark of shame on her chest."

"A wise statement!" the stranger commented, solemnly nodding his head. "This way she will serve as a living lesson against sin, until that shameful letter is carved upon her gravestone. It troubles me, however, that the man who shared in her wrongdoing should not, at the very least, stand on the platform beside her. But he will be discovered!—he will be discovered!—he will be discovered!"

He politely bowed to the talkative local resident, and after whispering a few words to his Native American companion, they both pushed their way through the crowd.

While this was happening, Hester Prynne had been standing on her platform, her eyes still locked on the stranger with such intensity that during moments of deep focus, everything else in the world around her seemed to disappear, leaving only the two of them. A private meeting like that might have been even more terrifying than facing him now, as she did, with the blazing midday sun beating down on her face and illuminating her disgrace; with the red symbol of her shame pinned to her chest; with the child born from sin cradled in her arms; with an entire crowd gathered as if for a celebration, all staring at features that should only have been seen in the gentle glow of a fireplace, in the comfort of a happy home, or hidden beneath a modest veil at church. As awful as her situation was, she found some protection in having all these thousands of people watching. It was better to stand here like this, with so many people between him and her, than to face him alone, just the two of them. She took refuge, in a way, in this public humiliation, and feared the moment when this protection would be taken away from her. Lost in these thoughts, she barely noticed a voice speaking behind her until it had called her name several times in a loud and serious tone that everyone in the crowd could hear.

"Listen to me, Hester Prynne!" said the voice.

It had already been observed that directly above the platform where Hester Prynne stood was a type of balcony, or open gallery, attached to the meeting-house. This was the location from which proclamations were customarily made, surrounded by an assembly of magistrates, with all the ceremony that accompanied such public events in those times. Here, to observe the scene we are describing, sat Governor Bellingham himself, with four sergeants positioned around his chair, carrying halberds as an honor guard. He wore a dark feather in his hat, an embroidered border on his cloak, and a black velvet tunic underneath; a gentleman well along in years, with harsh experience etched into his wrinkles. He was well suited to serve as the leader and representative of a community that owed its beginning and advancement, and its current state of development, not to youthful impulses, but to the stern and disciplined energies of manhood, and the somber wisdom of age; achieving so much precisely because it imagined and hoped so little. The other prominent figures who surrounded the chief ruler were marked by a dignified bearing that belonged to an era when the structures of authority were felt to possess the sacred nature of Divine institutions. They were, without doubt, good men, just and wise. However, from the entire human race, it would not have been easy to choose the same number of wise and virtuous individuals who would be less capable of passing judgment on a wayward woman's heart, and untangling its web of good and evil, than the stern-faced sages toward whom Hester Prynne now turned her gaze. She seemed aware, indeed, that whatever compassion she might expect lay in the broader and more generous heart of the crowd; for, as she raised her eyes toward the balcony, the unfortunate woman grew pale and trembled.

The voice that had caught her attention belonged to the respected and well-known John Wilson, Boston's senior clergyman, a distinguished scholar like most of his fellow ministers of that era, and also a man with a kind and warm-hearted nature. This final quality, though, had not been cultivated as carefully as his scholarly abilities, and was actually more a source of embarrassment than pride for him. There he stood, with a fringe of gray hair showing beneath his cap, while his pale eyes, used to the dim light of his private study, were squinting like those of Hester's baby in the bright, unfiltered sunlight. He resembled the somber engraved portraits that appear at the beginning of old sermon collections, and had no more business than one of those portraits would have had to emerge, as he was now doing, and interfere with matters involving human sin, desire, and suffering.

"Hester Prynne," said the clergyman, "I have been discussing with my young colleague here, under whose preaching you have had the privilege to sit"—here Mr. Wilson placed his hand on the shoulder of a pale young man beside him—"I have tried, I say, to convince this godly young man that he should confront you here before Heaven, and in front of these wise and righteous leaders, and within hearing of all the people, regarding the wickedness and darkness of your sin. Since he knows your natural disposition better than I do, he could better determine what arguments to use, whether gentle or harsh, that might overcome your stubbornness and defiance, so that you would no longer conceal the name of the man who led you to this terrible downfall. But he argues against me (with a young man's excessive gentleness, though he is wise beyond his years) that it would violate the very essence of womanhood to force her to reveal her heart's secrets in such public view and before such a large crowd. Indeed, as I tried to persuade him, the shame lies in committing the sin, not in revealing it. What do you say to this, once more, Brother Dimmesdale? Must it be you or I who deals with this poor sinner's soul?"

The distinguished and respected people sitting in the balcony began to murmur among themselves; and Governor Bellingham voiced what they were thinking, speaking with authority, though he showed respect for the young minister he was addressing.

"Good Master Dimmesdale," he said, "the responsibility for this woman's soul rests heavily with you. It is therefore your duty to urge her to repent and to confess, as proof and consequence of that repentance."

The directness of this request turned everyone's attention to Reverend Mr. Dimmesdale, a young minister who had arrived from one of England's prestigious universities, bringing with him all the knowledge of his time to this untamed wilderness. His powerful speaking ability and deep religious passion had already shown promise of great distinction in his calling. He possessed a remarkably striking appearance, featuring a pale, high, and prominent forehead, large brown eyes filled with sadness, and lips that trembled unless he deliberately held them firm, revealing both emotional sensitivity and tremendous inner discipline. Despite his natural talents and scholarly achievements, this young minister carried himself with a certain quality—a worried, startled, somewhat fearful expression—like someone who felt completely lost and confused about his place in human life, finding comfort only in solitude. As a result, whenever his responsibilities allowed, he chose quiet, hidden paths and maintained a simple, innocent nature; emerging when needed with such fresh, sweet, and pure thoughts that many people claimed his words affected them like the voice of an angel.

The young man standing before them was the one Reverend Mr. Wilson and the Governor had brought forward so publicly, asking him to speak before everyone about the mystery of a woman's soul—something sacred even when corrupted. The difficult nature of his situation drained the color from his face and caused his lips to shake.

"Talk to the woman, my brother," said Mr. Wilson. "This matters for her soul, and therefore, as the honorable Governor says, it's crucial for your own soul too, since you're responsible for hers. Urge her to confess the truth!"

The Reverend Mr. Dimmesdale lowered his head in what appeared to be silent prayer, then stepped forward.

"Hester Prynne," he said, leaning over the balcony and looking down steadily into her eyes, "you hear what this good man says, and you see the responsibility I'm working under. If you feel it would bring peace to your soul, and that your earthly punishment would become more effective for your salvation, I urge you to speak the name of your fellow sinner and fellow sufferer! Don't stay silent out of some misguided pity and tenderness for him; because, believe me, Hester, even if he had to step down from his high position and stand there beside you on your platform of shame, it would still be better than hiding a guilty heart for the rest of his life. What can your silence do for him, except tempt him—yes, practically force him—to add hypocrisy to his sin? Heaven has given you public disgrace so that you might achieve a public victory over the evil within you and the sorrow around you. Be careful not to deny him—who perhaps doesn't have the courage to grasp it himself—the bitter but healing cup that is now being offered to your lips!"

The young pastor's voice trembled with sweetness, rich and deep yet broken. The emotion it clearly expressed, more than the actual meaning of his words, resonated within every heart and united the listeners in shared sympathy. Even the infant at Hester's breast felt this same power, turning its previously unfocused gaze toward Mr. Dimmesdale and raising its tiny arms with a sound that was half content, half sorrowful. The minister's plea seemed so compelling that the crowd felt certain Hester Prynne would reveal the name of the guilty man, or that the guilty person himself, wherever he might be standing whether in high or humble position, would be pulled forward by some inner and unavoidable force, driven to climb up onto the scaffold.

Hester shook her head.

"Woman, do not go beyond the boundaries of God's mercy!" shouted Reverend Mr. Wilson, speaking more severely than he had before. "That little baby has been blessed with a voice to support and validate the advice you have received. Say the name! That, along with your repentance, might be enough to remove the scarlet letter from your chest."

"Never!" Hester Prynne replied, looking not at Mr. Wilson, but into the deep and troubled eyes of the younger clergyman. "It is too deeply burned into me. You cannot take it off. And I wish I could bear his suffering, as well as my own!"

"Speak, woman!" said another voice, coldly and sternly, coming from the crowd gathered around the scaffold. "Speak; and give your child a father!"

"I will not speak!" Hester replied, her face turning deathly pale as she responded to the voice she recognized all too well. "And my child must look to a heavenly Father; she will never know an earthly one!"

"She won't speak!" whispered Mr. Dimmesdale, who had been leaning over the balcony with his hand pressed against his heart, waiting to see how his plea would turn out. He stepped back now, taking a deep breath. "What incredible strength and nobility in a woman's heart! She won't speak!"

Recognizing the hopeless condition of the poor woman's mental state, the senior minister, who had thoroughly prepared for this moment, delivered a sermon to the crowd about sin in all its forms, constantly referring to the shameful letter. He focused so intensely on this symbol throughout the hour or more that his words washed over the people, causing the letter to take on new horrors in their minds and appear to draw its red color from the fires of hell itself. Hester Prynne, meanwhile, remained in her position on the platform of disgrace, her eyes vacant and her manner showing exhausted indifference. She had endured that morning everything that human nature could bear; and since she was not the type of person who escapes overwhelming suffering by fainting, her spirit could only protect itself behind a hard shell of numbness, while her basic physical functions continued normally. In this condition, the preacher's voice boomed mercilessly but uselessly in her ears. The baby, during the final part of her punishment, filled the air with its cries and screams; she tried to quiet it automatically, but seemed barely aware of its distress. With the same cold expression, she was escorted back to prison and disappeared from public view behind its iron-reinforced door. Those who watched her leave whispered that the scarlet letter cast an eerie glow along the dark hallway inside.

Chapter 4: The Interview.

After returning to the prison, Hester Prynne was discovered in a state of nervous agitation that required continuous supervision to prevent her from harming herself or causing some frantic injury to her poor infant. As evening drew near, and it became clear that her defiance could not be controlled through scolding or threats of punishment, Master Brackett, the jailer, decided it was appropriate to bring in a physician. He described this man as someone skilled in all Christian methods of medical science, and also knowledgeable about whatever the native people could teach regarding medicinal herbs and roots that grew in the wilderness. To be honest, there was great need for professional help, not only for Hester herself, but even more urgently for the child; who, receiving nourishment from her mother's breast, appeared to have absorbed along with it all the chaos, anguish and despair that filled the mother's body. The infant now twisted in spasms of pain, and represented in its tiny body a powerful symbol of the moral torment that Hester Prynne had endured throughout the day.

Right behind the jailer into the gloomy cell came that man with the unusual appearance, whose presence in the crowd had so deeply affected the woman wearing the scarlet letter. He was being held in the prison not because he was suspected of any crime, but because it was the most practical and appropriate way to house him while the magistrates discussed his ransom with the Indian chiefs. His name was given as Roger Chillingworth. After bringing him into the room, the jailer lingered for a moment, amazed by the sudden silence that followed his arrival; Hester Prynne had instantly become as motionless as death, though the child kept crying.

"Please, friend, leave me alone with my patient," said the doctor. "Trust me, good jailer, you will soon have peace in your house; and I promise you, Mistress Prynne will from now on be more cooperative with lawful authority than you may have found her before."

"No, if you can manage that," replied Master Brackett, "I'll acknowledge you as a truly skilled man! Indeed, the woman has been like someone possessed; and it wouldn't take much for me to decide to drive Satan out of her with a whipping."

The stranger had entered the room with the quiet manner typical of the profession he claimed to belong to. His behavior didn't change when the prison guard left, leaving him alone with the woman who had watched him so intently from the crowd, suggesting a close connection between them. He first attended to the child, whose cries as she twisted on the small bed made it absolutely necessary to calm her before doing anything else. He examined the baby thoroughly, then opened a leather case he had taken from under his clothing. The case seemed to hold medical supplies, and he mixed one of them with a cup of water.

"My previous studies in alchemy," he remarked, "and my stay for more than a year among people who understand the healing properties of medicinal plants, have made me a better doctor than many who hold medical degrees. Here, woman! The child belongs to you—she is not mine—and she will not recognize my voice or appearance as that of a father. Therefore, give her this medicine with your own hand."

Hester pushed away the medicine he offered, while staring at his face with clearly visible fear.

"Would you take revenge on an innocent baby?" she whispered.

"Foolish woman!" the doctor replied, his tone half cold, half comforting. "What reason would I have to harm this unfortunate and suffering baby? The medicine will do good, and if this were my own child—yes, my very own, just as much as yours—I couldn't do anything better for it."

As she continued to hesitate, being truly in no sound state of mind, he took the baby in his arms and gave the medicine himself. It quickly showed its effectiveness and fulfilled the doctor's promise. The little patient's moans quieted; its spasmodic movements slowly stopped; and within a few moments, as young children typically do after pain relief, the child fell into a deep and peaceful sleep. The physician, as he rightfully could be called, then turned his attention to the mother. With steady and focused examination, he checked her pulse and looked into her eyes—a stare that made her heart contract and tremble, because it felt so familiar yet so strange and distant—and finally, satisfied with his assessment, began to prepare another dose of medicine.

"I don't know about Lethe or Nepenthe," he said, "but I've discovered many new secrets in the wilderness, and here's one of them—a formula that a Native American taught me in exchange for some lessons of my own that were as ancient as Paracelsus. Drink this! It might not be as comforting as a clear conscience. I can't give you that. But it will settle the surge and turmoil of your emotions, like oil poured on the waves of a stormy sea."

He offered the cup to Hester, who took it while gazing slowly and seriously into his face; it wasn't exactly a fearful look, but one filled with uncertainty and questions about what he might be planning. She also glanced at her sleeping child.

"I have thought about death," she said, "I have wished for it—I would have even prayed for it, if it were appropriate for someone like me to pray for anything. But if death is in this cup, I ask you to think again before you watch me drink it. Look! It is right now at my lips."

"Drink, then," he replied, still with the same cold composure. "Do you know me so little, Hester Prynne? Are my purposes usually so shallow? Even if I imagine a scheme of vengeance, what could I do better for my goal than to let you live—than to give you medicines against all harm and danger of life—so that this burning shame may still blaze upon your chest?" As he spoke, he laid his long forefinger on the scarlet letter, which immediately seemed to burn into Hester's breast, as if it had been red-hot. He noticed her involuntary gesture, and smiled. "Live, therefore, and carry your fate with you, in the eyes of men and women—in the eyes of him whom you called your husband—in the eyes of that child over there! And, so that you may live, drink this potion."

Without any further argument or hesitation, Hester Prynne emptied the cup completely, and following the doctor's gesture, sat down on the bed where her child lay sleeping; meanwhile, he pulled over the room's only chair and positioned himself beside her. She couldn't help but shake at these arrangements; she sensed that—having now completed everything that compassion or duty, or perhaps even a sophisticated form of cruelty, had driven him to do for alleviating physical pain—he was about to confront her as the man she had wounded most profoundly and beyond repair.

"Hester," he said, "I'm not asking why or how you fell into this pit, or rather, how you climbed onto this platform of shame where I found you. The reason isn't hard to find. It was my foolishness and your weakness. I was a man of thought, someone who spent his life buried in the books of great libraries, a man already deteriorating, having given my best years to chase the endless dream of knowledge. What business did I have with youth and beauty like yours! Deformed from the moment I was born, how could I fool myself into thinking that intellectual abilities might hide physical ugliness in a young woman's imagination! People call me wise. If wise men were ever truly wise when it came to their own interests, I might have seen all this coming. I might have realized that when I emerged from that vast and gloomy forest and entered this community of Christian people, the very first thing I would see would be you, Hester Prynne, standing there like a monument to disgrace before everyone. In fact, from the moment we walked down those old church steps together as husband and wife, I might have seen the flames of that scarlet letter burning at the end of our journey!"

"You know," said Hester—for, depressed as she was, she could not endure this last quiet stab at the symbol of her shame—"you know that I was honest with you. I felt no love, nor pretended any."

"True," he replied. "It was my foolishness! I have admitted it. But up until that point in my life, I had been living without purpose. The world had felt so joyless! My heart was a dwelling spacious enough for many visitors, but it remained empty and cold, lacking the warmth of a home. I yearned to create that warmth! It didn't seem like such an impossible dream—despite my age, my darkness, and my deformity—that the simple happiness scattered everywhere for all people to claim might still become mine. And so, Hester, I brought you into my heart, into its deepest chamber, and tried to give you warmth through the heat that your presence created there!"

"I have deeply wronged you," whispered Hester.

"We have hurt each other," he replied. "I was the first to do wrong when I led your young life into a false and unnatural relationship with my old age. Therefore, as a man who has thought and reflected meaningfully, I don't seek revenge or plan any harm against you. Between you and me, things are evenly balanced. But, Hester, there's a man alive who has wronged us both! Who is he?"

"Don't ask me!" Hester Prynne replied, looking directly into his face with determination. "You will never know that!"

"Never, you say?" he replied, with a smile of dark and self-confident intelligence. "Never know him! Believe me, Hester, there are few things—whether in the physical world, or, to a certain extent, in the invisible realm of thought—few things hidden from the man who dedicates himself earnestly and completely to solving a mystery. You may hide your secret from the curious crowd. You may conceal it, too, from the ministers and magistrates, just as you did today, when they tried to force the name from your heart, and give you a companion on your platform of shame. But, as for me, I approach this investigation with different abilities than they have. I will search for this man, as I have searched for truth in books; as I have searched for gold in alchemy. There is a connection that will make me aware of him. I will see him tremble. I will feel myself shudder, suddenly and without warning. Sooner or later, he must inevitably be mine!"

The elderly scholar's eyes burned so intensely as he stared at her that Hester Prynne pressed her hands against her heart, terrified he might immediately discover the secret hidden there.

"You won't reveal his name? He's still mine regardless," he continued, with a look of confidence, as if fate were on his side. "He doesn't wear a letter of shame sewn into his clothing like you do, but I'll read it in his heart. But don't fear for him! Don't think that I'll interfere with Heaven's own way of punishment, or hurt myself by turning him over to human law. And don't imagine that I'll plot anything against his life; no, nor against his reputation, if he's a man of good standing, as I believe he is. Let him live! Let him hide behind outward respectability if he can! He'll still be mine!"

"Your actions seem merciful," Hester said, confused and horrified. "But your words make you sound terrifying!"

"One thing, you who were once my wife, I must ask of you," the scholar continued. "You have kept your lover's secret. Keep mine as well! No one in this land knows who I am. Do not tell any living person that you ever called me husband! Here, on this remote edge of the world, I will make my home; for though I have been a wanderer elsewhere, cut off from human connections, I find here a woman, a man, a child, among whom and myself there exist the strongest bonds. It doesn't matter whether those bonds are of love or hate; it doesn't matter whether they are right or wrong! You and yours, Hester Prynne, belong to me. My home is wherever you are, and wherever he is. But do not betray me!"

"Why do you want this?" Hester asked, pulling back, though she barely understood why she felt so uneasy about this secret agreement. "Why don't you reveal yourself publicly and be done with me once and for all?"

"It may be," he replied, "because I will not face the dishonor that stains the husband of an unfaithful woman. It may be for other reasons. Enough—it is my intention to live and die unknown. Let your husband be to the world as one already dead, and from whom no news shall ever come. Do not acknowledge me, by word, by gesture, by glance! Do not reveal the secret, above all, to the man you know of. Should you fail me in this, beware! His reputation, his position, his life, will be in my hands. Beware!"

"I will keep your secret, just as I have kept his," said Hester.

"Swear it!" he replied.

And she took the oath.

"And now, Mistress Prynne," said old Roger Chillingworth, as he would be called from then on, "I leave you alone; alone with your infant, and the scarlet letter! How is it, Hester? Does your sentence require you to wear the token even in your sleep? Are you not afraid of nightmares and hideous dreams?"

"Why are you smiling at me like that?" Hester asked, disturbed by the look in his eyes. "Are you like the Black Man who haunts the forest around us? Have you lured me into an agreement that will destroy my soul?"

"Not your soul," he replied, smiling again. "No, not yours!"

Chapter 5: Hester At Her Needle.

Hester Prynne's period of imprisonment had come to an end. Her prison door was flung open, and she stepped out into the sunlight, which, shining down on everyone equally, seemed to her troubled and tormented heart as though it existed solely to expose the scarlet letter on her chest. There was perhaps greater agony in her first solitary steps away from the prison entrance than even in the procession and public display that had been described earlier, where she had been made into a shared disgrace for all humanity to condemn. During that earlier ordeal, she had been sustained by an unnatural heightening of her nerves and by all the fighting spirit within her character, which allowed her to transform the scene into a kind of dark victory. It had also been a single, isolated event that would happen only once in her life, and to face it, she could recklessly spend all the vital energy that might have lasted her through many peaceful years. The very law that had condemned her—like a stern-faced giant with the strength in his iron grip both to support and to destroy—had upheld her through the terrible trial of her public shame. But now, with this solitary walk from her prison door, the daily routine began, and she would have to either endure and continue forward using only her natural strength, or collapse under the weight. She could no longer steal from tomorrow to help her bear today's sorrow. The next day would bring its own ordeal, as would the day after that, and the one following; each would have its own trial, yet it would be exactly the same one that was now so unbearably painful to endure. The days stretching into the distant future would march forward, still carrying the same burden for her to pick up and carry with her, but never to cast aside; for the mounting days and accumulating years would add their suffering to the pile of disgrace. Through all of them, surrendering her individual identity, she would become the universal symbol that preachers and moral teachers could point to, and through which they could bring to life and give form to their representations of women's weakness and sinful desire. This is how the young and innocent would be taught to view her, with the scarlet letter blazing on her chest—her, the daughter of respectable parents—her, the mother of an infant who would one day become a woman—her, who had once been pure—as the symbol, the physical form, the living embodiment of sin. And above her grave, the disgrace that she must carry there would be her only memorial.

It might seem amazing that, with the entire world open to her—not bound by any restrictive terms of her punishment to stay within the limits of the Puritan settlement, so distant and so hidden—free to return to her birthplace, or to any other European country, and there conceal her character and identity beneath a new appearance, as completely as if stepping into another existence—and having also the pathways of the dark, mysterious forest available to her, where the wildness of her nature might blend itself with a people whose customs and way of life were foreign to the law that had condemned her—it might seem amazing that this woman should still consider that place her home, where, and only where, she must inevitably be the symbol of shame. But there exists a destiny, a feeling so compelling and unavoidable that it carries the power of fate, which almost always forces human beings to linger around and haunt, like ghosts, the place where some great and significant event has shaped their entire life; and even more compellingly when the experience that marks it is darker. Her sin, her disgrace, were the roots she had planted deep in the ground. It was as if a rebirth, with stronger connections than the first, had transformed the forest-land, still so unwelcoming to every other pilgrim and wanderer, into Hester Prynne's wild and bleak, but lifelong home. All other places on earth—even that village of rural England, where happy childhood and pure young womanhood seemed still to remain in her mother's care, like clothes set aside long ago—were foreign to her by comparison. The chain that held her here was made of iron links, and painful to her deepest soul, but could never be broken.

It might also be true—and it certainly was, though she

concealed this secret from herself and turned pale whenever it emerged from her heart like a snake from its den—that another emotion kept her in this place and on this path that had brought such tragedy. Here lived and walked the man with whom she believed herself joined in a bond that, though unacknowledged on earth, would unite them before the throne of final judgment and transform that moment into their wedding altar for an eternal future of endless punishment. Again and again, the tempter of souls had forced this thought into Hester's mind and mocked the passionate and desperate joy with which she grasped it before struggling to push it away. She could barely face this idea directly and quickly moved to lock it away in its prison. What she forced herself to believe—what she ultimately convinced herself was her reason for remaining in New England—was part truth and part self-deception. Here, she told herself, had been the place of her sin, and here should be the place of her earthly punishment; and perhaps the agony of her daily shame would eventually cleanse her soul and create a different kind of purity than what she had lost—one more holy because it came through suffering.

The Lonesome Dwelling

Hester Prynne, therefore, did not run away. On the edge of the town, within the boundaries of the peninsula, but not close to any other dwelling, there stood a small cottage with a thatched roof. An earlier settler had built it and then abandoned it because the soil around it was too barren for farming, while its relative isolation placed it outside the circle of social activity that already characterized the settlers' way of life. The cottage sat on the shore, gazing across a stretch of sea toward the forest-covered hills in the west. A cluster of scraggly trees, the only kind that grew on the peninsula, didn't really hide the cottage from sight but rather seemed to suggest that here was something that wanted to be hidden, or at least should have been hidden. In this small, isolated home, using what little money she had and with permission from the magistrates, who continued to keep a watchful eye on her, Hester made her home with her baby. An air of mysterious suspicion immediately settled over the place. Children, too young to understand why this woman should be excluded from human kindness, would creep close enough to watch her sewing at the cottage window, or standing in the doorway, or working in her small garden, or walking along the path that led toward town; and when they spotted the scarlet letter on her chest, they would run away with a strange, infectious fear.

Despite Hester's isolation and having no friend on earth who dared to reveal themselves, she faced no danger of poverty. She possessed a skill that was sufficient, even in a land that offered relatively little opportunity for its practice, to provide food for both her thriving infant and herself. This skill was needlework—then, as now, almost the only craft within a woman's reach. She wore on her chest, in the intricately embroidered letter, an example of her delicate and creative ability, which court ladies would have gladly used to add the richer and more spiritual decoration of human craftsmanship to their silk and gold fabrics. Here, indeed, in the dark simplicity that generally marked Puritan clothing styles, there might be rare demand for the finer products of her handiwork. Yet the taste of the era, requiring whatever was elaborate in works of this type, did not fail to extend its influence over our strict ancestors, who had abandoned so many customs which might seem harder to give up. Public ceremonies, such as ordinations, the installation of magistrates, and everything that could give dignity to the forms in which a new government showed itself to the people, were, as a matter of policy, marked by a stately and well-organized ceremonial, and a somber, but still a deliberate magnificence. Deep ruffs, carefully crafted bands, and splendidly embroidered gloves, were all considered necessary to the official status of men taking control of power; and were readily permitted to individuals distinguished by rank or wealth, even while sumptuary laws prohibited these and similar luxuries to the common people. In funeral arrangements, too—whether for the clothing of the deceased body, or to represent, through various symbolic designs of black cloth and white linen, the grief of the survivors—there was a frequent and distinctive demand for such work as Hester Prynne could provide. Baby clothing—for infants then wore ceremonial robes—offered yet another opportunity for labor and payment.

Gradually, and quite quickly, her needlework became what we would now call fashionable. Whether people sought her services out of pity for a woman with such a tragic fate, or from the unhealthy fascination that gives artificial worth even to ordinary or worthless items, or because of whatever other mysterious factors that were then, as they are now, enough to grant some people what others might desperately seek, or simply because Hester truly filled a need that would otherwise have gone unmet—whatever the reason, she certainly had steady and well-paid work for as many hours as she chose to spend with her needle. Perhaps vanity chose to humble itself by wearing, during grand ceremonies and official events, clothing that had been created by her sinful hands. Her needlework appeared on the Governor's collar; soldiers wore it on their sashes, and ministers on their clerical bands; it adorned babies' little caps; it was sealed away to grow moldy and decay in the coffins of the dead. But there is no record that even once her skill was requested to embroider the white veil meant to cover a bride's innocent blushes. This single exception revealed the unforgiving harshness with which society condemned her transgression.

Hester didn't try to get anything more than the bare necessities for survival, choosing the plainest and most austere lifestyle for herself, while providing simple comfort for her child. She wore clothes made from the roughest fabrics in the darkest colors, with only one decoration—the scarlet letter—which she was condemned to display. Her child's clothing, however, showed creative and imaginative skill that we might even call fantastical, which enhanced the delicate charm that began to emerge in the little girl early on, but this seemed to carry a deeper significance as well. We'll discuss this more later. Apart from this small expense on decorating her baby, Hester gave all her extra money to charity, helping people who were less unfortunate than she was, and who often showed contempt for the very person who helped them. She spent much of the time that she could have used to create better artistic work making rough clothes for poor people instead. There was probably an element of self-punishment in this type of work, and she likely made a real sacrifice of pleasure by dedicating so many hours to such crude needlework. She naturally had a rich, sensual, exotic quality—an appreciation for magnificent beauty, which, except for the exquisite work she created with her needle, had no other outlet in all the possibilities her life offered. Women find a pleasure in the delicate work of sewing that the opposite sex cannot understand. For Hester Prynne, this might have been a way to express, and therefore calm, the deepest feelings of her life. Like all other pleasures, she rejected it as sinful. This unhealthy interference of conscience with something that didn't really matter suggested, we should worry, not genuine and lasting repentance, but something questionable, something that might be seriously wrong underneath.

In this way, Hester Prynne found herself with a role to play in the world. With her natural strength of character and exceptional abilities, society could not completely reject her, even though it had marked her with a burden more unbearable to a woman's heart than the mark that branded Cain's forehead. In all her dealings with society, however, nothing made her feel like she truly belonged to it. Every gesture, every word, and even the silence of those she encountered suggested, and often openly stated, that she was an outcast, as isolated as if she lived in another world, or connected to ordinary human nature through different organs and senses than the rest of humanity. She remained separate from moral concerns, yet stayed close to them, like a spirit that returns to a familiar home but can no longer be seen or felt; unable to share in the family's happiness or grieve with their sorrows; or, if it managed to show its forbidden compassion, it would only inspire fear and terrible disgust. These feelings, along with the harshest contempt, seemed to be the only share she had left in the collective human heart. It was not a time of sensitivity; and her situation, though she understood it clearly and was unlikely to forget it, was often thrust into her sharp awareness, like fresh pain, by the cruelest touch on her most vulnerable spot. The poor people, as we have mentioned, whom she tried to help with her charity, often cursed the hand that reached out to assist them. Women of high social standing, whose homes she entered for her work, were used to dropping bitter poison into her heart; sometimes through that process of quiet cruelty by which women can create deadly venom from ordinary small things; and sometimes through harsher words that struck the victim's unprotected heart like a brutal blow on an infected wound. Hester had trained herself long and thoroughly; she never fought back against these attacks, except for a flush of red that rose uncontrollably across her pale face, then sank back into the depths of her chest. She was patient—truly a martyr—but she held back from praying for her enemies; worried that, despite her forgiving intentions, the words of blessing might stubbornly turn themselves into a curse.

Constantly, and in countless other ways, she felt the endless waves of pain that had been so cleverly designed for her by the relentless, ever-present judgment of the Puritan court. Ministers would stop her on the street to offer words of moral instruction, which drew crowds with their mixed sneers and disapproval around the unfortunate, sinful woman. When she entered a church, hoping to share in the Sabbath blessing of the Universal Father, she often found herself becoming the subject of the sermon. She developed a fear of children, as they had absorbed from their parents a confused sense of something terrible about this somber woman who moved quietly through the town with no companion except her single child. So they would first let her pass, then follow her from a distance with piercing shouts and words that held no clear meaning in their young minds, but were nonetheless horrifying to her because they came from lips that spoke them without understanding. This seemed to show how widely her shame had spread—that all of nature was aware of it. It could not have caused her deeper pain if the leaves on the trees had whispered her dark story among themselves, if the summer wind had murmured about it, or if the winter storm had screamed it out loud! Another unique form of torture came from the stare of unfamiliar eyes. When strangers looked with curiosity at the scarlet letter—and they all inevitably did—they burned it fresh into Hester's soul, so that she could barely stop herself, though she always managed to stop herself, from covering the symbol with her hand. But then again, a familiar eye brought its own suffering. Its cold stare of recognition was unbearable. From beginning to end, in summary, Hester Prynne always experienced this terrible agony whenever she felt human eyes upon the mark; the spot never became numb; instead, it seemed to grow more painful with each day's torment.

Lonely Footsteps

But sometimes, once every few days, or perhaps after many months had passed, she sensed an eye—a human eye—looking at the shameful mark, which seemed to provide a brief moment of relief, as though half of her suffering had been shared with another. The very next moment, all the pain came flooding back with an even deeper wave of anguish; because, in that short moment, she had committed a fresh sin. Had Hester been the only one to sin?

Her imagination was somewhat affected, and if she had been of a gentler moral and intellectual nature, would have been even more so, by the strange and isolated anguish of her life. Walking back and forth, with those solitary footsteps, in the small world to which she was outwardly connected, it sometimes seemed to Hester—if it was entirely fantasy, it was nevertheless too powerful to be resisted—she felt or imagined, then, that the scarlet letter had given her a new sense. She trembled to believe, yet could not help believing, that it granted her an intuitive knowledge of the hidden sin in other hearts. She was terrified by the revelations that were thus made. What were they? Could they be anything other than the cunning whispers of the evil angel, who would gladly have convinced the struggling woman, as yet only half his victim, that the outward appearance of purity was nothing but a lie, and that, if truth were everywhere to be revealed, a scarlet letter would burn bright on many a chest besides Hester Prynne's? Or, must she accept those hints—so vague, yet so clear—as truth? In all her wretched experience, there was nothing else so terrible and so disgusting as this sense. It confused, as well as shocked her, by the disrespectful inappropriateness of the occasions that brought it into sharp focus. Sometimes the red disgrace upon her chest would give a sympathetic pulse, as she passed near a respected minister or magistrate, the model of devotion and justice, to whom that age of ancient reverence looked up, as to a mortal man in fellowship with angels. "What evil thing is nearby?" would Hester say to herself. Raising her unwilling eyes, there would be nothing human within sight, except the form of this earthly saint! Again, a mysterious sisterhood would defiantly assert itself, as she met the holy frown of some matron, who, according to the gossip of all voices, had kept cold snow within her chest throughout life. That unsunned snow in the matron's chest, and the burning shame on

Hester Prynne's—what did the two have in common? Or, once more, the electric shock would give her warning—"Look, Hester, here is a companion!"—and, glancing up, she would catch the eyes of a young maiden looking at the scarlet letter, timidly and sideways, and quickly turned away with a faint, cold crimson in her cheeks; as if her purity were somewhat tainted by that brief glance. O Devil, whose charm was that fatal symbol, would you leave nothing, whether in youth or age, for this poor sinner to respect?—such loss of faith is always one of the saddest results of sin. Let it be accepted as proof that all was not corrupt in this poor victim of her own weakness, and man's harsh law, that Hester Prynne still struggled to believe that no fellow human was guilty like herself.

The common people, who in those grim old days always added a disturbing and frightening element to whatever captured their imagination, had a tale about the scarlet letter that we could easily develop into a terrifying legend. They claimed that the symbol was not simply scarlet fabric dyed in an ordinary dye-pot, but was blazing hot with hellish fire, and could be seen glowing brightly whenever Hester Prynne walked outside at night. And we must acknowledge that it burned Hester's chest so profoundly that perhaps there was more truth in the rumor than our modern skepticism might be willing to accept.

Vignette

Chapter 6: Pearl

We have barely mentioned the infant so far; that small creature whose innocent life had emerged, through providence's mysterious will, as a beautiful and eternal flower from the wild growth of a sinful passion. How remarkable it seemed to the sorrowful woman as she observed the child's development, the beauty that grew more radiant each day, and the intelligence that cast its shimmering light across this little one's delicate features! Her pearl!—this was what Hester had named her; not because the name reflected her appearance, which possessed none of the serene, white, emotionless glow that such a comparison would suggest. Instead, she called the infant "pearl" because she was of immense value—bought with everything she possessed—her mother's sole treasure! How remarkable, truly! Mankind had branded this woman's transgression with a scarlet letter, which carried such powerful and devastating force that no human compassion could reach her, unless it came from someone equally sinful. God, as a direct result of the sin that mankind had punished in this way, had blessed her with a beautiful child, whose rightful place was upon that same disgraced chest, linking her mother eternally to the human family and lineage, and destined to become a blessed spirit in paradise! Still, these reflections filled Hester Prynne more with fear than with hope. She understood that her actions had been wicked; therefore, she could not believe that their outcome would be virtuous. Each day, she anxiously studied the child's developing character, constantly fearing she might discover some dark and untamed trait that would match the guilt from which the child's existence sprang.

There was certainly nothing wrong with her physically. With her perfect form, vitality, and natural skill in using all her untested limbs, the baby deserved to have been born in Eden itself—deserved to have remained there as a plaything for the angels after the world's first parents were cast out. The child possessed an inborn elegance that doesn't always accompany flawless beauty; her clothing, no matter how simple, always struck observers as the exact outfit that suited her best. But little Pearl wasn't dressed in plain country clothes. Her mother, driven by a disturbing obsession that will become clearer later, had purchased the finest fabrics available and given her creative imagination free rein in designing and decorating the dresses the child wore in public. The small figure looked so magnificent when dressed this way, and Pearl's own natural beauty shone so brilliantly through these splendid garments that might have overwhelmed a less radiant loveliness, that she seemed surrounded by an actual circle of light on the dim cottage floor. Yet even a brown dress, torn and dirty from the child's rough play, created an equally perfect image of her. Pearl's appearance was touched with a magic of endless variation; within this single child existed many children, spanning the complete range from the wildflower charm of a peasant baby to the miniature grandeur of a royal infant. Through all these transformations, however, ran a thread of intensity, a certain richness of character, which she never lost; and if she had ever become dimmer or more pale in any of her changes, she would have stopped being herself—she would no longer have been Pearl!

This external changeability reflected, and accurately expressed, the diverse qualities of her inner nature. Her character seemed to have depth as well as complexity; but—unless Hester's worries misled her—it lacked connection and adjustment to the world she had been born into. The child could not be brought under control of regulations. In creating her life, a fundamental law had been violated; and the outcome was a person whose traits were possibly beautiful and radiant, but completely chaotic; or following a pattern unique to themselves, within which the principle of diversity and organization was hard or impossible to find. Hester could only explain the child's personality—and even then very uncertainly and incompletely—by remembering what she herself had experienced during that crucial time while Pearl was absorbing her spirit from the ethereal realm, and her physical body from earthly matter. The mother's intense emotional condition had served as the channel through which the elements of moral existence were passed to the developing child; and, no matter how pure and transparent they had been originally, they had absorbed the deep colors of red and gold, the blazing brightness, the dark shadows, and the harsh light of the medium they passed through. Most importantly, the conflict within Hester's soul during that time was carried forward in Pearl. She could identify her own wild, frantic, rebellious feelings, the unpredictability of her emotions, and even some of the exact formations of sadness and despair that had settled in her heart. They were now brightened by the morning glow of a young child's nature, but later in life's journey might give rise to turbulence and chaos.

Family discipline in those days was much stricter than it is today. Parents regularly used stern looks, harsh scolding, and frequent beatings—all supported by Biblical teachings—not just to punish children for wrongdoing, but as a healthy routine to encourage good behavior and moral development. However, Hester Prynne, raising this one child alone, was unlikely to be too harsh in her approach. Still aware of her own mistakes and troubles, she tried early on to establish gentle but firm guidance over the young soul entrusted to her care. But this proved to be beyond her abilities. After trying both kindness and sternness, and finding that neither approach had any predictable effect, Hester eventually had to step back and let the child follow her own instincts. Physical force or restraint worked, naturally, while it was being applied. As for any other type of discipline, whether aimed at her mind or emotions, little Pearl might or might not respond to it, depending on whatever whim controlled her at the time. While Pearl was still a baby, her mother became familiar with a particular expression that warned her when it would be pointless to insist, convince, or beg. This look was so intelligent yet mysterious, so stubborn, sometimes so mischievous, but usually paired with wild energy, that Hester couldn't help wondering in those moments whether Pearl was actually a human child. She seemed more like a magical fairy who, after playing her imaginative games briefly on the cottage floor, would dart away with a teasing smile. Whenever that expression appeared in her wild, bright, deep black eyes, it gave her a strange distance and untouchable quality; it was as though she were floating in the air and might disappear, like a flickering light that appears from nowhere and vanishes to nowhere. Seeing this, Hester felt compelled to rush toward the child—to chase the little fairy as she inevitably began to flee—to grab her and hold her close with tight embraces and passionate kisses—not so much from overwhelming love, but to convince herself that Pearl was real flesh and blood, and not completely imaginary. But Pearl's laughter when she was caught, though filled with joy and melody, left her mother feeling even more uncertain than before.

Heartbroken by this confusing and puzzling enchantment that so often came between her and her only treasure, whom she had paid for so dearly and who was her entire world, Hester sometimes broke into passionate tears. Then, perhaps—for there was no predicting how it might affect her—Pearl would scowl and clench her little fist, hardening her small features into a stern, unsympathetic expression of displeasure. Often, she would laugh again, louder than before, like something incapable and unaware of human sorrow. Or—though this happened more rarely—she would be overcome with furious grief and sob out her love for her mother in broken words, seeming determined to prove she had a heart by breaking it. Yet Hester could hardly feel safe trusting in that stormy tenderness; it vanished as suddenly as it appeared. Thinking about all these things, the mother felt like someone who had summoned a spirit but, through some mistake in the conjuring process, had failed to discover the magic word that should control this new and mysterious intelligence. Her only true comfort came when the child lay in peaceful sleep. Then she was certain of her and enjoyed hours of quiet, sad, wonderful happiness—until, perhaps with that mischievous expression flickering beneath her opening eyelids, little Pearl woke up!

How quickly—with what remarkable speed, really!—Pearl reached an age where she could interact socially, beyond her mother's constant smile and baby talk! And what joy it would have brought if Hester Prynne could have heard her clear, songbird-like voice mixing with the noise of other children's voices, and could have picked out and recognized her own beloved child's sounds among all the tangled shouts of a group of playing children! But this could never happen. Pearl was born an outcast from the world of children. A little devil, a symbol and result of sin, she had no place among baptized babies. Nothing was more striking than the instinct, it appeared, with which the child understood her isolation; the fate that had drawn an unbreakable circle around her; the complete strangeness, in other words, of her situation compared to other children. Never, since leaving prison, had Hester faced the public eye without her. On all her walks through the town, Pearl was there too; first as the baby in her arms, and later as the little girl, her mother's small companion, gripping one finger with her entire hand, and walking along at a pace of three or four steps to each one of Hester's. She watched the settlement's children, on the grassy edge of the street, or at doorsteps of homes, playing in the stern way that Puritan upbringing allowed; perhaps pretending to go to church; or whipping Quakers; or taking scalps in pretend battles with Indians; or frightening each other with acts of make-believe witchcraft. Pearl observed, and stared closely, but never tried to make friends. If someone spoke to her, she wouldn't speak back. If the children gathered around her, as they sometimes did, Pearl would become truly frightening in her small rage, grabbing stones to throw at them, with sharp, meaningless cries that made her mother shake, because they sounded so much like a witch's curses in some foreign language.

The reality was that these small Puritans, belonging to the most narrow-minded group that had ever existed, had developed a unclear sense of something foreign, supernatural, or conflicting with normal customs in the mother and child; consequently, they despised them in their minds and frequently attacked them with harsh words. Pearl sensed this attitude and responded with the most intense hatred that could be imagined to fester in a young child's heart. These explosions of fierce anger held a certain worth, and even provided solace, for her mother; since there was at least an understandable intensity in this behavior, rather than the unpredictable whims that so often frustrated her in the child's actions. It frightened her, however, to recognize here, once more, a faint echo of the wickedness that had existed within herself. All this hostility and fury Pearl had inherited, by undeniable birthright, from Hester's heart. Mother and daughter existed together within the same boundary of isolation from human society; and in the child's character seemed to continue those restless forces that had troubled Hester Prynne before Pearl's birth, but had since started to be calmed by the gentle effects of motherhood.

At home, in and around her mother's cottage, Pearl didn't need a large and diverse group of friends. The magic of life flowed from her endlessly creative spirit and spread to countless objects, like a torch lighting a flame wherever it touches. The most unlikely materials—a stick, a bundle of rags, a flower—became the actors in Pearl's enchantment, and without any visible change, they became spiritually suited to whatever story was playing out in her inner world. Her single baby voice gave life to numerous imaginary characters, both old and young, for her to speak with. The pine trees, ancient, dark and serious, casting groans and other sad sounds into the wind, needed little change to represent Puritan elders; the ugliest weeds in the garden became their children, whom Pearl struck down and pulled up without mercy. It was amazing to see the incredible variety of forms her mind could take, with no real pattern, but jumping up and dancing, always in a state of supernatural activity—soon falling down as if worn out by such a quick and fevered rush of life—and then replaced by other forms of similar wild energy. It was like nothing more than the ghostly display of the northern lights. In simply using her imagination and the playfulness of a developing mind, there might have been little more than what could be seen in other children with bright abilities; except that Pearl, lacking human playmates, relied more heavily on the imaginary crowd she created. What made her unique was the unfriendly feelings the child had toward all these creations of her own heart and mind. She never made a friend, but always seemed to be scattering the dragon's teeth everywhere, from which grew a crop of armed enemies that she rushed to fight. It was impossibly sad—and what deep grief for a mother who felt the reason in her own heart!—to see in someone so young this constant awareness of a hostile world, and such fierce preparation of the strength that would be needed to defend her position in the battle that was sure to come.

Looking at Pearl, Hester Prynne often let her work fall to her lap and cried out in anguish that she wanted to hide but couldn't contain, somewhere between speaking and groaning, "O Father in Heaven—if You are still my Father—what is this child that I have brought into the world!" And Pearl, hearing this outburst or sensing through some deeper awareness her mother's waves of pain, would turn her bright and beautiful little face toward her mother, smile with an almost supernatural intelligence, and go back to her playing.

A Touch of Pearl's Baby Hand

There's still one more strange aspect of the child's behavior that needs to be mentioned. The very first thing she noticed in her life was—what exactly?—not her mother's smile, which would have prompted her to respond like other babies do, with that faint, beginning smile of her tiny mouth that parents remember so uncertainly afterward, debating fondly whether it was truly a smile at all. Not at all! Instead, the first thing that Pearl seemed to become aware of was—should we admit it?—the scarlet letter on Hester's chest! One day, when her mother leaned over the cradle, the baby's eyes were drawn to the shimmer of the gold embroidery around the letter; reaching up with her small hand, she grabbed for it, smiling not uncertainly, but with a clear brightness that made her face appear much older than her years. Then, struggling to breathe, Hester Prynne seized the cursed symbol, instinctively trying to pull it away; the pain caused by Pearl's baby hand touching it with such awareness was unbearable. Again, as though her mother's distressed reaction was simply meant to entertain her, little Pearl looked directly into her eyes and smiled! From that moment on, except when the child was sleeping, Hester never experienced a single moment of peace; not one moment of relaxed happiness with her daughter. Sometimes weeks would pass during which Pearl's attention might never focus on the scarlet letter; but then it would return unexpectedly, like a sudden fatal blow, and always accompanied by that distinctive smile and strange look in her eyes.

Once, this strange, otherworldly expression appeared in the child's eyes while Hester was gazing at her own reflection in them, as mothers love to do; and suddenly—for women who are alone and troubled are plagued by inexplicable visions—she imagined that she saw not her own tiny image, but another face in the small dark mirror of Pearl's eye. It was a demonic face, filled with cruel amusement, yet it resembled features she knew very well, though she had rarely seen them smile, and never with such cruelty. It seemed as though an evil spirit had taken hold of the child and was peering out mockingly at that moment. Many times afterward, Hester had been tormented by this same vision, though never quite as clearly.

On a summer afternoon, after Pearl had grown old enough to run around, she entertained herself by collecting handfuls of wildflowers and throwing them one by one at her mother's chest, jumping up and down like a small fairy each time she struck the scarlet letter. Hester's immediate reaction was to shield her chest with her folded hands. However, whether driven by pride, acceptance, or the belief that her punishment would be best fulfilled through this unbearable suffering, she fought against this urge and remained sitting upright, pale as a corpse, gazing sorrowfully into little Pearl's untamed eyes. The assault of flowers continued, almost always finding their target and covering the mother's breast with wounds for which she could discover no healing in this world, nor did she understand how to find it in the next. Finally, when the child had used up all her ammunition, she stopped and stared at Hester, with that small, mocking image of a demon looking out—or whether it truly appeared or not, her mother believed she saw it—from the mysterious depths of her dark eyes.

"Child, what are you?" cried the mother.

"Oh, I am your little Pearl!" the child replied.

But as she spoke these words, Pearl laughed and started dancing up and down with the playful gestures of a little imp who might decide to fly up the chimney as her next mischievous trick.

"Are you truly my child?" asked Hester.

She didn't ask the question carelessly, but in that moment, with some real seriousness; Pearl's remarkable intelligence was such that her mother wondered if she might already know the hidden truth about her own existence and could reveal it now.

"Yes; I am little Pearl!" the child repeated, continuing her playful antics.

"You are not my child! You are no Pearl of mine!" said the mother, half playfully; for it was often the case that a playful impulse came over her, in the midst of her deepest suffering. "Tell me, then, what you are, and who sent you here."

"Tell me, mother!" the child said seriously, walking up to Hester and pressing herself close to her knees. "Please tell me!"

"Your Heavenly Father sent you!" answered Hester Prynne.

But she spoke with a hesitation that the sharp-eyed child didn't miss. Whether driven simply by her usual mischievous nature, or because some wicked impulse urged her on, she raised her small index finger and touched the scarlet letter.

"He didn't send me!" she cried emphatically. "I don't have a Heavenly Father!"

"Quiet, Pearl, quiet! You mustn't talk like that!" answered the mother, holding back a groan. "He sent us all into this world. He sent even me, your mother. Then, much more, you! Or, if not, you strange and otherworldly child, where did you come from?"

"Tell me! Tell me!" Pearl repeated, no longer serious, but laughing and dancing around the floor. "You're the one who has to tell me!"

But Hester couldn't answer the question, finding herself trapped in her own maze of uncertainty. She recalled—with both a smile and a shiver—the gossip from people in nearby towns who had searched unsuccessfully for the child's father and, noticing some of Pearl's strange qualities, had declared that poor little Pearl was the child of a demon. According to their beliefs, such children had appeared on earth from time to time since the old Catholic era, born through their mother's sin and meant to serve some evil and corrupt purpose. Luther, if we believe the malicious rumors spread by his monk enemies, was supposedly one of these children from hell, and Pearl wasn't the only child among the New England Puritans to be given such an unfortunate origin story.

Chapter 7: The Governor's Hall.

One day, Hester Prynne visited governor Bellingham's mansion, carrying a pair of gloves she had decorated with fringe and embroidery according to his specifications, gloves intended for some important state ceremony; although the unpredictable nature of popular elections had caused this former leader to fall from the highest position of power, he still maintained a respected and influential role among the colonial officials.

Another and much more important reason than delivering a pair of embroidered gloves drove Hester, at this time, to seek a meeting with someone who held so much power and influence in the settlement's affairs. She had heard that some of the leading residents, who held the strictest religious and governmental principles, were planning to take her child away from her. Based on the assumption that Pearl was of demonic origin, as already suggested, these well-meaning people reasonably argued that concern for the mother's soul required them to remove such an obstacle from her path. If the child, on the other hand, was truly capable of moral and religious development, and possessed the potential for ultimate salvation, then surely she would have a much better chance of achieving these benefits by being placed under wiser and better care than Hester Prynne could provide. Among those who supported this plan, Governor Bellingham was said to be one of the most active. It may seem strange, and even somewhat ridiculous, that a matter of this type, which in later times would have been handled by no higher authority than the town's selectmen, was then a subject of public debate, with prominent statesmen taking sides. During that era of original simplicity, however, issues of even less public concern, and far less real importance, than the welfare of Hester and her child, were oddly entangled with legislative discussions and government actions. The time period was barely, if at all, before our story, when a disagreement about property rights to a pig not only sparked a fierce and bitter fight in the colony's legislative body, but also led to a significant change in the legislature's very structure.

Filled with worry, yet so aware of her own righteousness that it felt like a fair fight between the public on one side and a solitary woman supported by nature's compassion on the other, Hester Prynne left her isolated cottage. Little Pearl naturally came with her. She was now old enough to run easily alongside her mother, and being constantly active from morning until evening, she could have managed a much longer trip than the one ahead of them. Still, often more from whim than need, she insisted on being picked up and carried; but soon she would just as stubbornly demand to be put down again, and would skip ahead of Hester on the grass-covered path, with many innocent stumbles and falls. We have mentioned Pearl's abundant and striking beauty; a beauty that glowed with rich and vibrant colors; a radiant complexion, eyes that held both deep intensity and bright sparkle, and hair that was already a deep, shining brown, which in later years would become almost black. There was energy in her and all around her; she appeared to be the spontaneous result of a moment of passion. Her mother, when designing the child's clothing, had given her imagination complete freedom; dressing her in a crimson velvet dress with an unusual design, heavily decorated with elaborate patterns and ornaments made of gold thread. Such bold coloring, which would have made paler children look sickly and washed out, perfectly suited Pearl's beauty, and made her the most brilliant little spark of fire that ever moved across the earth.

But there was something extraordinary about this outfit, and really about the child's entire appearance, that powerfully and unavoidably brought to mind the symbol that Hester Prynne was condemned to wear on her chest. It was the scarlet letter transformed into another shape; the scarlet letter brought to life! The mother herself—as though the red shame had been burned so deeply into her mind that everything she imagined took on its appearance—had carefully created this resemblance; spending countless hours of unhealthy creativity to forge a connection between the person she loved and the symbol of her shame and suffering. But in reality, Pearl embodied both meanings; and it was only because of this dual nature that Hester had managed to so perfectly mirror the scarlet letter in her daughter's appearance.

As the two travelers entered the town limits, the Puritan children looked up from their games—or what counted as games for those serious little children—and spoke solemnly to one another:

"Look, there's the woman with the scarlet letter; and truly, there's the image of the scarlet letter running alongside her! Come on, let's throw mud at them!"

But Pearl, who was a fearless child, after scowling, stomping her foot, and waving her small hand with various threatening movements, suddenly charged at the group of her enemies and sent them all running. In her fierce chase after them, she looked like a young plague—scarlet fever, or some similar half-formed angel of punishment—whose purpose was to make the next generation pay for their sins. She also screamed and yelled with such tremendous volume that it undoubtedly made the hearts of those fleeing shake with fear. Once she had won, Pearl calmly walked back to her mother and looked up at her face with a smile.

Without any further incident, they arrived at Governor Bellingham's home. This was a large wooden house, constructed in a style that can still be seen in examples throughout the streets of our older towns today; now covered with moss, falling apart, and filled with sadness from the many sorrowful or joyful events, both remembered and forgotten, that have taken place and faded away within their dim rooms. At that time, however, the building had the freshness of recent construction on its outside, and the warmth that shone from the bright windows of a home where death had never set foot. The house had a very cheerful appearance; the walls were covered with a type of plaster mixed generously with pieces of broken glass, so that when sunlight struck the front of the building at an angle, it gleamed and sparkled as though handfuls of diamonds had been thrown against it. This brilliance would have been more fitting for Aladdin's palace than for the home of a serious old Puritan leader. The house was also decorated with unusual and seemingly mystical symbols and patterns, matching the distinctive style of that era, which had been carved into the plaster while it was still wet and had since hardened permanently for future generations to admire.

Pearl, gazing at this magnificent house that seemed to glow with wonder, started jumping and dancing around, demanding that all the bright sunlight covering the front of the building should be peeled away and handed over to her as a plaything.

"No, my little Pearl!" said her mother. "You must find your own happiness. I have none to give you!"

They walked up to the door, which had an arched shape and was bordered on both sides by narrow towers that jutted out from the building. Each tower had lattice windows with wooden shutters that could be closed when necessary. Hester Prynne lifted the iron knocker that hung at the entrance and knocked, and one of the Governor's servants answered—a man born free in England but now serving as a slave for seven years. During this time, he belonged to his master and could be bought and sold like an ox or a piece of furniture. The servant wore a blue coat, which was the standard uniform for serving men of that era, and had been for many years before in the old ancestral halls of England.

"Is the honorable Governor Bellingham inside?" asked Hester.

"Yes, indeed," replied the servant, staring with wide-open eyes at the scarlet letter, which, being a newcomer to the country, he had never seen before. "Yes, his honorable worship is inside. But he has a godly minister or two with him, and also a doctor. You may not see his worship right now."

"Even so, I will go in," Hester Prynne replied, and the servant, perhaps deciding from her determined manner and the gleaming symbol on her chest that she was an important woman in the community, did not try to stop her.

So the mother and little Pearl were allowed into the entrance hall. With many changes suggested by the nature of his building materials, the different climate, and a distinct way of social living, Governor Bellingham had designed his new home based on the houses of well-to-do gentlemen in his homeland. Here, then, was a broad and fairly high-ceilinged hall that stretched through the entire depth of the house and served as a central pathway connecting, more or less directly, with all the other rooms. At one end, this large room was lit by the windows of the two towers, which created a small alcove on each side of the entrance. At the other end, though partially hidden by a curtain, it was more brightly lit by one of those bay windows with curved glass that we read about in old books, and which had a deep, cushioned window seat. There, on the cushion, lay a large book, probably the Chronicles of England or other such weighty literature; just as, in our own time, we place decorative books on the coffee table for visitors to browse through. The hall's furniture included some heavy chairs with backs that were intricately carved with designs of oak flowers, along with a table in the same style; all of it from the Elizabethan era or perhaps even earlier, and family treasures brought here from the Governor's ancestral home. On the table—as a sign that the tradition of old English hospitality had not been forgotten—sat a large pewter mug, at the bottom of which, if Hester or Pearl had looked inside, they would have seen the foamy remains of a recently consumed beer.

On the wall hung a series of portraits depicting the ancestors of the Bellingham family line, some wearing armor across their chests, while others displayed elaborate ruffs and formal robes of peacetime. Each portrait shared the harsh and severe expression that old paintings so consistently display, as though they were spirits rather than mere images of deceased dignitaries, staring down with stern and unforgiving judgment at the activities and pleasures of the living.

The Governor's Breastplate

At the center of the oak panels that lined the hall hung a suit of armor, not an ancestral relic like the paintings, but of the most recent design; it had been crafted by a skilled armorer in London during the same year that Governor Bellingham arrived in New England. The suit included a steel helmet, a breastplate, a throat guard, and leg armor, along with a pair of metal gloves and a sword hanging below; all pieces, particularly the helmet and chest plate, were polished so brilliantly that they glowed with white light and cast illumination across the floor around them. This gleaming armor wasn't intended merely for display, but had been worn by the Governor during numerous formal military gatherings and training exercises, and had also shone at the front of a regiment during the Pequod war. Although trained as a lawyer and accustomed to citing Bacon, Coke, Noye, and Finch as his professional colleagues, the demands of this new land had transformed Governor Bellingham into a soldier as well as a statesman and leader.

Little Pearl—who was just as delighted with the shining armor as she had been with the sparkling decorative front of the house—spent some time gazing into the polished mirror-like surface of the breastplate.

"Mother," she cried out, "I can see you here. Look! Look!"

Hester glanced over to humor her daughter and noticed that the curved mirror's unusual properties made the scarlet letter appear enormously magnified, transforming it into the most striking aspect of her reflection. She seemed completely overshadowed by it. Pearl also pointed up at a similar image in the helmet's decorative piece, grinning at her mother with that mischievous cleverness that had become such a characteristic expression on her little face. That playful, impish look was also captured in the mirror, but with such amplified intensity that it made Hester Prynne feel as though she wasn't looking at her own child's reflection, but rather at some sprite trying to take on Pearl's form.

"Come on, Pearl," she said, pulling her away. "Come and look at this beautiful garden. Maybe we'll see flowers there that are more beautiful than the ones we find in the woods."

Pearl ran to the large window at the far end of the hall and gazed down the length of a garden path covered with neatly trimmed grass and lined with a crude and undeveloped attempt at landscaping. However, the owner seemed to have already given up hope of recreating the traditional English love for decorative gardening on this side of the Atlantic, where the soil was harsh and people struggled just to survive. Cabbages grew openly in view, and a pumpkin vine that had taken root some distance away had spread across the space between, placing one of its enormous fruits directly under the hall window—as though warning the Governor that this massive piece of vegetable gold was the finest decoration the New England soil could provide him. There were a few rose bushes, though, along with several apple trees that were likely descendants of those planted by Reverend Mr. Blackstone, the peninsula's first settler—that semi-legendary figure who appears throughout our early historical records riding on the back of a bull.

Pearl spotted the rose bushes and started crying for a red rose, refusing to be comforted.

"Quiet, child, quiet!" her mother said urgently. "Don't cry, dear little Pearl! I can hear voices in the garden. The Governor is approaching, and there are gentlemen with him!"

In reality, several people could be seen walking down the garden path toward the house. Pearl, completely dismissing her mother's efforts to calm her, let out an eerie shriek and then fell silent; not because she intended to obey, but because her quick and restless curiosity was stirred by the sight of these new arrivals.

Chapter 8: The Elf-Child And The Minister.

Governor Bellingham, wearing a loose robe and comfortable cap—the kind that elderly gentlemen liked to put on when relaxing at home in private—walked at the front of the group, and seemed to be showing off his property while discussing his planned improvements. The wide circle of an ornate ruff beneath his gray beard, styled in the old-fashioned way from King James's time, made his head look quite similar to that of John the Baptist on a platter. The impression created by his appearance, so stiff and stern, and withered by more than the usual aging of autumn, hardly matched the luxurious comforts he had clearly tried his best to surround himself with. But it would be wrong to think that our serious ancestors—even though they were used to speaking and thinking of human life as simply a time of testing and struggle, and even though they were genuinely ready to give up possessions and life when duty demanded it—believed it was morally wrong to accept whatever comfort or even luxury they could reasonably obtain. This belief was never preached, for example, by the respected pastor John Wilson, whose beard, white as fresh snow, could be seen over Governor Bellingham's shoulder; while he suggested that pears and peaches might eventually grow well in New England's climate, and that purple grapes could possibly be made to flourish against the sunny garden wall. The old minister, raised in the wealthy tradition of the English Church, had a well-established and proper appreciation for all good and comfortable things; and no matter how strict he might appear in the pulpit, or when publicly condemning sins like Hester Prynne's, the kind warmth of his private life had earned him deeper affection than any of his fellow clergymen received.

Behind the Governor and Mr. Wilson came two other guests: one was the Reverend Arthur Dimmesdale, whom readers may recall as having played a brief and reluctant role in the scene of Hester Prynne's public shame; and walking closely beside him was old Roger Chillingworth, a man of great medical skill who had been living in the town for the past two or three years. It was widely known that this scholarly man served as both physician and friend to the young minister, whose health had been seriously damaged recently by his excessive devotion to the work and responsibilities of his pastoral duties.

The Governor walked ahead of his guests, climbed one or two steps, and pushed open the large hall window doors to find himself standing right next to little Pearl. The curtain's shadow fell across Hester Prynne, partially hiding her from view.

"What do we have here?" said Governor Bellingham, staring with surprise at the small scarlet figure standing before him. "I must say, I haven't seen anything like this since my days of vanity, back in old King James's time, when I used to consider it a great honor to be invited to a court masquerade! There would be crowds of these little creatures during the holidays, and we called them children of the Lord of Misrule. But how did such a visitor get into my hall?"

"Yes, indeed!" exclaimed good old Mr. Wilson. "What little

bird with scarlet feathers might this be? I think I have seen such figures when the sun has been shining through a richly painted window, casting golden and crimson images across the floor. But that was in the old country. Please tell me, young one, who are you, and what has caused your mother to dress you in this strange way? Are you a Christian child? Do you know your catechism? Or are you one of those mischievous elves or fairies that we thought we had left behind us, along with other remnants of Catholic practices, in merry old England?"

"I am my mother's child," replied the scarlet figure, "and my name is Pearl!"

"Pearl? Ruby, more like it! Or Coral! Or Red Rose, at the very least, judging by your coloring!" the old minister replied, reaching out his hand in a futile attempt to pat little Pearl on the cheek. "But where is your mother? Ah! I see," he continued, and turning to Governor Bellingham, he whispered, "This is the very same child we've been discussing; and look, here is the unfortunate woman, Hester Prynne, her mother!"

"Is that what you're saying?" the Governor exclaimed. "Well, we might have guessed that such a child's mother would have to be a sinful woman, a perfect example of the whore of Babylon! But she arrives at just the right time, and we'll investigate this matter immediately."

Governor Bellingham walked through the window into the hall, with his three guests following behind him.

"Hester Prynne," he said, fixing his naturally stern gaze on the woman wearing the scarlet letter, "there has been much discussion about you lately. The question has been seriously debated whether we, who hold positions of authority and influence, can in good conscience trust an immortal soul, such as exists in that child over there, to the care of someone who has stumbled and fallen among the temptations of this world. Speak up, as the child's own mother! Don't you think it would be better for your little one's earthly and eternal well-being if she were removed from your care, dressed modestly, disciplined strictly, and taught the truths of heaven and earth? What can you possibly do for the child in this regard?"

"I can teach my little Pearl what I have learned from this!" answered Hester Prynne, placing her finger on the red symbol.

"Woman, that letter is your mark of disgrace!" the harsh magistrate responded. "It's because of the sin that letter represents that we want to place your child with other people."

"Still," the mother said calmly, though her face was growing paler, "this badge has taught me—it teaches me every day—it's teaching me right now—lessons that might make my child wiser and better, even though they can't help me at all."

"We will make our decision carefully," said Bellingham, "and think thoroughly about what we're going to do. Good Master Wilson, I ask you to examine this Pearl—since that's her name—and see whether she has received the kind of Christian upbringing that's appropriate for a child her age."

The elderly minister settled into an armchair and tried to pull Pearl between his knees. However, the child, who wasn't used to being touched or treated familiarly by anyone except her mother, slipped away through the open window and stood on the top step, resembling a wild tropical bird with brilliant feathers, ready to fly up into the sky. Mr. Wilson, quite surprised by this sudden reaction—since he was a grandfatherly type of person who was usually very popular with children—nevertheless attempted to continue with the questioning.

"Pearl," he said with deep seriousness, "you must pay attention to your lessons, so that when the time comes, you can carry the pearl of great price in your heart. Can you tell me, my child, who created you?"

Now Pearl knew perfectly well who had created her; Hester Prynne, who came from a devout household, had started teaching her daughter about these spiritual truths very soon after their conversation about her Heavenly Father. The human soul, no matter how young and undeveloped, absorbs such knowledge with tremendous enthusiasm. Pearl had learned so much during her three short years of life that she could have easily passed a test on the New England Primer or the first section of the Westminster Catechisms, even though she had never actually seen either of these famous religious texts. However, that stubborn streak that exists in all children to some degree, and which little Pearl possessed ten times over, suddenly took complete control of her at this most inappropriate moment, either sealing her lips shut or driving her to say the wrong things entirely. After sticking her finger in her mouth and rudely refusing multiple times to answer good Mr. Wilson's question, the child finally declared that she hadn't been created at all, but instead had been picked by her mother from the wild rosebush that grew beside the prison door.

This fantasy was likely inspired by the Governor's red roses growing close by, as Pearl stood outside the window, combined with her memory of the rose bush at the prison, which she had walked past on her way here.

Old Roger Chillingworth, wearing a smile on his face, whispered something into the young minister's ear. Hester Prynne gazed at the learned man, and even at that moment, with her destiny hanging in the balance, she was shocked to notice what a transformation had occurred in his appearance—how much more hideous his features had become—how his dark skin seemed to have grown even darker, and his body more deformed—since the time when she had known him intimately. She caught his eyes for a brief moment, but was immediately forced to focus all her attention on the events now unfolding before her.

"This is terrible!" exclaimed the Governor, gradually recovering from the shock that Pearl's answer had caused him. "Here we have a three-year-old child, and she can't even say who created her! Without a doubt, she's just as ignorant about her soul, its current sinful state, and what awaits her in the future! I think, gentlemen, we don't need to ask any more questions."

Hester grabbed Pearl and pulled her firmly into her arms, facing the elderly Puritan magistrate with an almost fierce look. Standing alone in the world, rejected by society, with only this precious child to keep her heart beating, she felt she had undeniable rights that no one could take away, and she was prepared to fight for them until her last breath.

"God gave me this child!" she cried out. "He gave her to me as compensation for everything else you had taken away from me. She is my joy—but she is also my agony! Pearl keeps me alive! Pearl also punishes me! Don't you see, she is the scarlet letter itself, only capable of being loved, and blessed with a million times the power to make me pay for my sin? You will not take her from me! I would rather die first!"

"Make sure of it! I will not lose the child!"

"My poor woman," said the old minister, who wasn't unkind, "the child will be well taken care of—much better than you could manage!"

"God gave her into my keeping," Hester Prynne repeated, raising her voice almost to a shriek. "I will not give her up!" And here, driven by a sudden impulse, she turned to the young clergyman, Mr. Dimmesdale, at whom, up to this moment, she had seemed hardly to direct her eyes even once. "Speak for me!" she cried. "You were my pastor, and had charge of my soul, and know me better than these men can. I will not lose the child! Speak for me! You know—for you have sympathies which these men lack—you know what is in my heart, and what a mother's rights are, and how much stronger they are when that mother has only her child and the scarlet letter! See to it! I will not lose the child! See to it!"

At this wild and unusual plea, which showed that Hester Prynne's circumstances had driven her nearly to madness, the young minister immediately stepped forward, pale, and pressing his hand against his heart, as he always did whenever his particularly anxious nature became disturbed. He appeared more worn down and thin than when we saw him during Hester's public humiliation; and whether it was his declining health, or whatever else might be the reason, his large dark eyes contained a universe of suffering in their troubled and sorrowful depths.

"There is truth in what she says," the minister began, his voice sweet, trembling, but powerful, so much so that the hall echoed, and the hollow armor resonated with it—"truth in what Hester says, and in the feeling that drives her! God gave her the child, and also gave her an instinctive understanding of its nature and needs—both apparently so unique—which no other human being can have. And furthermore, isn't there a quality of profound sacredness in the relationship between this mother and this child?"

"Yes! How is that, good Master Dimmesdale?" interrupted the Governor. "Make that clear, I beg you!"

"It must be so," the minister continued. "If we think otherwise, aren't we saying that the Heavenly Father, the Creator of all people, has carelessly overlooked a sinful act and ignored the difference between unholy lust and sacred love? This child, born from its father's guilt and its mother's shame, has come from God's hand to work in many ways upon the heart of she who pleads so desperately, and with such anguish of spirit, for the right to keep her. It was intended as a blessing; as the one blessing of her life! It was intended, no doubt, as the mother herself has told us, as punishment too; a torment to be felt at many unexpected moments; a sharp pain, a sting, a constantly returning agony, in the middle of troubled joy! Has she not expressed this thought in the clothing of the poor child, so powerfully reminding us of that red symbol which burns upon her chest?"

"Excellent point, once again!" exclaimed the kind Mr. Wilson. "I was worried the woman had no better idea than to turn her child into a circus performer!"

"Oh, no—not at all!" Mr. Dimmesdale went on. "She understands, believe me, the sacred miracle that God has created through this child's existence. And she may also feel—what I believe is the absolute truth—that this gift was intended, more than anything else, to keep the mother's soul alive and to save her from the darker depths of sin that Satan might otherwise have tried to drag her into! That's why it's beneficial for this poor, sinful woman to have an infant with an immortal soul, a being capable of eternal happiness or suffering, entrusted to her care—to be raised by her in righteousness—to remind her, every single moment, of her downfall—but also to show her, as if through the Creator's holy promise, that if she guides the child to heaven, the child will also bring its parent there! In this way, the sinful mother is more fortunate than the sinful father. For Hester Prynne's sake, then, and equally for the poor child's sake, let us leave them as Providence has chosen to place them!"

"You're speaking with unusual intensity, my friend," said old Roger Chillingworth, smiling at him.

"And there is significant meaning in what my young colleague has said," added Reverend Mr. Wilson. "What do you think, honorable Master Bellingham? Has he not argued well for this unfortunate woman?"

"He certainly has," replied the magistrate, "and he has presented such compelling arguments that we will leave the matter as it currently stands, at least as long as there is no further scandal involving the woman. Nevertheless, we must ensure that the child receives proper and regular instruction in the catechism, either from you or from Master Dimmesdale. Furthermore, when the time is right, the tithing-men must make sure that she attends both school and church services."

When the young minister finished speaking, he stepped back a few paces from the group and stood with his face partly hidden behind the thick folds of the window curtain. The shadow of his figure, cast on the floor by the sunlight, trembled with the intensity of his passionate words. Pearl, that wild and unpredictable little sprite, quietly crept toward him and took his hand in both of hers, pressing her cheek against it. This gesture was so tender and yet so subtle that her mother, watching from nearby, wondered to herself, "Is that really my Pearl?" Still, she understood that love existed in the child's heart, even though it usually showed itself through fierce emotion, and perhaps only twice in her entire life had it been softened by such gentle affection as she displayed now. The minister—because aside from the long-desired attention of a woman, nothing is more precious than these signs of a child's favor, given freely through spiritual intuition and therefore seeming to suggest something genuinely lovable within us—the minister turned around, placed his hand on the child's head, paused for a moment, and then kissed her forehead. Little Pearl's unusual sentimental mood didn't last long. She burst into laughter and went skipping down the hallway so lightly that old Mr. Wilson wondered aloud whether her toes even touched the ground.

"The little girl has something magical about her, I swear," he said to Mr. Dimmesdale. "She doesn't need an old woman's broomstick to fly with!"

"What an unusual child!" old Roger Chillingworth observed. "You can easily see her mother's influence in her. Do you think, gentlemen, that it would be beyond a philosopher's ability to study that child's character and, based on her temperament and nature, make an educated guess about who her father might be?"

"No; it would be wrong, in such a matter, to follow the guidance of worldly philosophy," said Mr. Wilson. "It would be better to fast and pray about it; and perhaps even better to leave the mystery as we find it, unless God reveals it on His own. In this way, every good Christian man has the right to show a father's kindness toward the poor, abandoned child."

With the matter settled so successfully, Hester Prynne left the house with Pearl. As they walked down the steps, it's said that a bedroom window's lattice was suddenly thrown open, and Mistress Hibbins thrust her face out into the bright sunlight—Governor Bellingham's ill-tempered sister, the same woman who would be executed as a witch just a few years later.

"Listen, listen!" she said, while her ominous face seemed to cast a shadow over the cheerful newness of the house. "Will you come with us tonight? There will be a merry group in the forest; and I nearly promised the Black Man that beautiful Hester Prynne should join us."

"Please make my apologies to him!" Hester replied with a triumphant smile. "I need to stay home and watch over my little Pearl. If they had taken her away from me, I would have gladly gone with you into the forest and signed my name in the Black Man's book as well, using my own blood!"

"We'll have you there soon!" said the witch-lady, frowning as she pulled back her head.

But here—if we assume this conversation between Mistress Hibbins and Hester Prynne actually happened, and wasn't just a symbolic story—we already had proof of the young minister's argument against separating a fallen mother from the child born of her weakness. Even this early, the child had saved her from Satan's trap.

Chapter 9: The Leech.

The reader will recall that beneath the name Roger Chillingworth lay concealed another identity, which the man who once bore it had determined should never again be uttered. We have already learned how, among the crowd that witnessed Hester Prynne's shameful public punishment, there stood an elderly, weary traveler who had just emerged from the dangerous wilderness and saw the woman in whom he had expected to find the warmth and joy of home now displayed before the people as a symbol of sin. Her reputation as a respectable wife had been trampled beneath everyone's feet. Disgrace surrounded her with gossip in the public square. For her relatives, should word ever reach them, and for those who had known her in her innocent life, nothing remained but the stain of her shame, which would surely spread in direct relation to how close and sacred their previous bonds with her had been. Why then—since the decision was his to make—should the person whose connection to this fallen woman had been the most intimate and sacred of all step forward to claim an inheritance so undesirable? He decided not to be displayed alongside her on her platform of shame. Known only to Hester Prynne and holding the key to her silence, he chose to remove his name from the records of humanity and, concerning his former relationships and concerns, to disappear from life as completely as if he truly rested at the bottom of the ocean, where rumors had long since placed him. Once this goal was accomplished, new interests would immediately arise, along with a new purpose—dark, certainly, if not sinful, but powerful enough to occupy all his mental abilities.

Following this decision, he settled in the Puritan town as Roger Chillingworth, bringing with him only the exceptional learning and intelligence he possessed in abundance. Since his earlier studies had given him extensive knowledge of contemporary medical science, he introduced himself as a physician and was warmly welcomed in that capacity. Skilled practitioners in medicine and surgery were extremely rare in the colony. It seemed they rarely shared the religious fervor that drove other emigrants to cross the Atlantic. Perhaps their investigations into the human body caused these men's higher and more refined abilities to become overly focused on material matters, causing them to lose sight of life's spiritual dimension while becoming absorbed in the complexities of that remarkable biological system, which appeared to contain enough intricacy to encompass all of existence. In any case, the health of the good town of Boston, insofar as medicine played a role, had previously been entrusted to an elderly deacon and apothecary, whose religious devotion and moral character served as stronger recommendations than any diploma he might have presented. The only surgeon was someone who occasionally practiced that distinguished profession while regularly wielding a barber's razor as his daily trade. Roger Chillingworth proved to be an outstanding addition to this limited medical community. He quickly demonstrated his expertise with the complex and impressive methods of traditional medicine, where each treatment included numerous exotic and diverse components, mixed together as intricately as if the intended outcome were the legendary Elixir of Life. Additionally, during his captivity among the Indians, he had acquired considerable understanding of the healing properties of local plants and roots. He openly told his patients that these natural remedies, which Nature had provided to indigenous peoples, earned just as much of his trust as the European medical knowledge that countless learned physicians had spent generations developing.

This educated newcomer was exemplary, at least when it came to the outward appearances of religious life, and shortly after his arrival, he had selected Reverend Mr. Dimmesdale as his spiritual guide. The young clergyman, whose scholarly reputation still flourished at Oxford, was regarded by his most passionate followers as nothing short of a divinely appointed apostle, destined, if he lived and worked for a normal lifespan, to accomplish as remarkable achievements for the currently weakened New England Church as the early Church Fathers had accomplished for the beginning of the Christian faith. Around this time, however, Mr. Dimmesdale's health had clearly started to deteriorate. Those most familiar with his daily routines attributed the pallor of the young minister's face to his overly intense dedication to study, his meticulous fulfillment of parish responsibilities, and, above all, to the fasting and nighttime prayers he frequently practiced in order to prevent the material concerns of this worldly existence from weighing down and dimming his spiritual light. Some proclaimed that if Mr. Dimmesdale was truly dying, it was reason enough that the world was unworthy to be walked upon by his feet any longer. He himself, conversely, with his typical modesty, expressed his conviction that if Providence chose to take him away, it would be due to his own inadequacy to carry out its most humble work here on earth. Despite all these differing opinions about the reason for his deterioration, the reality itself was undeniable. His body became gaunt; his voice, while still melodious and pleasant, carried a certain sorrowful hint of decline; he was frequently seen, whenever there was any minor disturbance or other unexpected incident, placing his hand over his heart, first flushing and then turning pale, showing signs of pain.

This was the young minister's situation, and the likelihood that his emerging promise would be snuffed out prematurely seemed very real, when Roger Chillingworth arrived in the town. His initial appearance on the scene—few people could say from where he came, seeming to drop down from the heavens or emerge from the depths of the earth—carried an air of mystery that could easily be elevated to the miraculous. He was now recognized as a skilled man; people noticed that he collected herbs and wild flower blossoms, dug up roots, and picked twigs from forest trees, like someone familiar with hidden properties in things that appeared worthless to ordinary observers. He was heard speaking of Sir Kenelm Digby and other renowned men—whose scientific achievements were considered almost supernatural—as having been his correspondents or colleagues. Why, with such standing in the scholarly world, had he come to this place? What could someone whose domain was in great cities be looking for in the wilderness? In response to this question, a rumor spread—and, though ridiculous, was believed by some very reasonable people—that Heaven had performed an absolute miracle by physically transporting a distinguished Doctor of Medicine from a German university through the air and placing him at the entrance of Mr. Dimmesdale's study! People of more sensible faith, however, who understood that Heaven accomplishes its goals without seeking the dramatic effect of what is called miraculous intervention, were inclined to see divine providence in Roger Chillingworth's perfectly timed arrival.

This idea was supported by the strong interest that the doctor always showed in the young minister; he became attached to him as a member of his congregation and tried to earn friendly regard and trust from his naturally guarded nature. He expressed great concern about his pastor's health, but was eager to attempt a cure, and if started early, he didn't seem pessimistic about achieving a positive outcome. The church elders, the deacons, the motherly women, and the young and beautiful unmarried women of Mr. Dimmesdale's congregation were all persistent in urging him to try the physician's openly offered expertise. Mr. Dimmesdale politely rejected their pleas.

"I don't need any medicine," he said.

But how could the young minister make such a claim when, with each passing Sunday, his face grew paler and more gaunt, and his voice became increasingly shaky—when it had become his regular habit, rather than an occasional gesture, to press his hand against his heart? Was he exhausted from his work? Did he want to die? These questions were seriously posed to Mr. Dimmesdale by the senior ministers of Boston and the deacons of his church, who, in their own words, "confronted him" about the sin of refusing the help that Providence so clearly offered. He listened without speaking, and eventually promised to consult with the physician.

"If it were God's will," said Reverend Mr. Dimmesdale, when he asked old Roger Chillingworth for his professional medical advice to fulfill this promise, "I would be perfectly content if my work, my sorrows, my sins, and my suffering would soon end with me, and whatever earthly part of them could be buried in my grave, while the spiritual part goes with me to my eternal state, rather than having you test your medical skills on my behalf."

"Ah," Roger Chillingworth responded with that calm demeanor that characterized all his behavior, whether it was genuine or put on, "that's exactly how a young minister tends to talk. Young men, who haven't yet established deep roots, give up on life so readily! And holy men, who walk alongside God here on earth, would eagerly prefer to leave this world behind to walk with Him on the golden streets of the New Jerusalem."

"No," the young minister replied, placing his hand over his heart as a flash of pain crossed his face, "if I were more worthy to walk there, I could find greater peace in working here."

"Good men always judge themselves too harshly," said the physician.

The Minister and Leech

In this way, the enigmatic old Roger Chillingworth became the medical advisor to Reverend Mr. Dimmesdale. Since the physician was interested not only in the illness but also felt compelled to examine the character and nature of his patient, these two men, so different in age, gradually began spending considerable time together. For the minister's health, and to allow the doctor to collect plants with healing properties, they took lengthy walks along the seashore or through the forest, mixing various conversations with the splash and whisper of the waves and the solemn wind-song among the treetops. Frequently, one would visit the other in his place of study and solitude. The minister found something captivating about the company of this man of science, in whom he recognized intellectual development of considerable depth and breadth, along with a range and liberty of thought that he would have searched for in vain among members of his own profession. Indeed, he was surprised, if not disturbed, to discover this quality in the physician. Mr. Dimmesdale was a genuine priest, a true believer, with deeply developed reverence and a type of mind that drove itself forcefully along the path of doctrine, wearing that passage continually deeper as time passed. In no society would he have been considered a man of progressive views; it would always be necessary for his peace of mind to feel the weight of faith surrounding him, supporting him while confining him within its rigid structure. Nevertheless, though with nervous pleasure, he did experience occasional relief in viewing the universe through a different kind of intellect than those with whom he usually conversed. It was as though a window had been flung open, letting fresher air into the cramped and suffocating study where his life was slowly deteriorating amid lamplight or blocked daylight and the stale scent, whether physical or spiritual, that rises from books. But the air was too fresh and cold to breathe comfortably for long. So the minister, along with the physician, retreated once more within the boundaries of what their church considered orthodox.

Roger Chillingworth carefully studied his patient, observing him both during his normal daily routine when he followed his usual patterns of thinking, and when he found himself in different moral situations that might reveal new aspects of his personality. Chillingworth believed it was crucial to truly understand the man before trying to help him. Whenever someone has both a heart and a mind, their physical ailments are influenced by the unique qualities of these inner aspects. In Arthur Dimmesdale's case, his thoughts and imagination were extremely active, and his sensitivity was so heightened, that any physical illness would likely have its roots in these mental and emotional factors. So Roger

Chillingworth—the skilled practitioner, the caring and supportive physician—worked to penetrate deeply into his patient's inner self, digging through his beliefs, examining his memories, and exploring everything with careful precision, like someone searching for treasure in a dark cave. Very few secrets can remain hidden from an investigator who has both the opportunity and permission to conduct such an exploration, along with the expertise to pursue it effectively. A person carrying a secret should particularly avoid becoming close to his doctor. If that doctor possesses natural wisdom and something else that's hard to define—let's call it intuition; if he doesn't display intrusive self-centeredness or unpleasantly obvious personal traits; if he has the ability, which must be an inborn gift, to align his mind so closely with his patient's that the patient unknowingly speaks aloud what he believes he has only thought; if such revelations are received calmly and acknowledged not so much through spoken sympathy as through silence, a quiet breath, and occasional words that show complete understanding; if these qualities of a trusted confidant are combined with the benefits that come from his established reputation as a physician—then, at some unavoidable moment, the sufferer's soul will dissolve and pour out like a dark but clear stream, exposing all its hidden truths to the light of day.

Roger Chillingworth had all, or nearly all, of the qualities mentioned above. Even so, time passed, and a certain closeness developed between these two educated men, as we've described. They had the entire realm of human thought and learning as common ground where they could connect. They discussed every subject related to ethics and religion, public matters and personal character. Both men spoke extensively about issues that seemed deeply personal to them. Yet no secret—the kind the physician believed must surely exist—ever slipped from the minister's mind into his companion's hearing. The doctor did suspect, however, that even the true nature of Mr. Dimmesdale's physical illness had never been honestly disclosed to him. What an unusual reluctance to share!

After some time, following a suggestion from Roger Chillingworth, Mr. Dimmesdale's friends arranged for the two men to live in the same house, ensuring that every rise and fall of the minister's health could be observed by his concerned and devoted physician. The entire town celebrated when this highly desired arrangement was achieved. Everyone believed it was the best possible solution for the young clergyman's well-being, unless he had chosen one of the many devoted young women who admired him spiritually to become his loving wife, as many people who felt they had the right to suggest often recommended. However, there was no immediate likelihood that Arthur Dimmesdale could be convinced to take this step; he dismissed all such proposals as if maintaining priestly celibacy was one of his fundamental religious principles. Since Mr. Dimmesdale had clearly chosen to condemn himself to always eating his bland meals at someone else's table and enduring the lifelong loneliness that comes to those who can only find warmth at another person's hearth, it truly appeared that this wise, experienced, and kind old physician, with his combination of fatherly and respectful affection for the young pastor, was exactly the right person to be constantly available whenever needed.

The two friends found their new home with a devout widow of respectable social standing, who lived in a house that occupied almost the exact location where the stately King's Chapel would later be constructed. The graveyard, which had originally been Isaac Johnson's home property, lay on one side of the house, making it perfectly suited to inspire the kind of serious contemplation that both the minister and the doctor needed for their respective work. The caring widow thoughtfully gave Mr. Dimmesdale a front room with windows facing the sun, complete with thick curtains that could create midday shade whenever he wanted it. Tapestries covered the walls all around the room, reportedly woven at the famous Gobelin workshops, depicting the Biblical tale of David and Bathsheba along with Nathan the Prophet in colors that remained bright and vivid, though they made the beautiful woman in the story appear almost as darkly striking as the prophet who proclaimed doom. In this room, the pale minister built up his impressive library, filled with leather-bound volumes containing the writings of the Church Fathers, Jewish scholarly works, and medieval religious scholarship—sources that Protestant clergy, despite publicly condemning and criticizing such authors, often found themselves forced to consult and use. On the opposite side of the house, old Roger Chillingworth set up his study and laboratory, which wouldn't meet the standards of a modern scientist for even basic completeness, but it came equipped with distillation equipment and the tools needed for mixing medicines and chemical compounds, instruments that the experienced alchemist understood perfectly how to use effectively. With such a convenient living arrangement, these two scholarly men settled into their respective spaces, each ruling over his own territory, yet regularly moving back and forth between the rooms and taking a mutual and quite interested look into each other's work.

The Reverend Arthur Dimmesdale's most perceptive friends, as we have suggested, quite reasonably believed that Providence had orchestrated all of this for the purpose—requested through countless public, private, and secret prayers—of restoring the young minister to good health. However—it must now be acknowledged—another segment of the community had recently begun to form its own opinion about the relationship between Mr. Dimmesdale and the enigmatic old physician. When an uneducated crowd tries to see with its own eyes, it is extremely likely to be misled. Yet when it forms its opinion, as it typically does, based on the instincts of its generous and passionate heart, the conclusions reached are often so deep and so accurate that they seem like divinely revealed truths. The people, in this particular situation, could not support their bias against Roger Chillingworth with any facts or reasoning worthy of serious consideration. There was an elderly craftsman, to be sure, who had lived in London during the time of Sir Thomas Overbury's murder, roughly thirty years earlier; he claimed to have seen the physician, under a different name that the storyteller had since forgotten, in the company of Doctor Forman, the renowned old sorcerer who was connected to the Overbury incident. A few people suggested that this learned man, during his captivity among the Indians, had expanded his medical knowledge by participating in the rituals of the native medicine men, who were widely recognized as powerful magicians, often achieving apparently miraculous healings through their mastery of dark arts. A significant number of people—many of whom possessed such sound judgment and keen observation that their views would have carried weight in other circumstances—declared that Roger Chillingworth's appearance had changed dramatically while he had lived in the town, particularly since he had taken up residence with Mr. Dimmesdale. Initially, his expression had been peaceful, thoughtful, and scholarly. Now, there was something repulsive and sinister in his face that they had not noticed before, and which became increasingly apparent each time they observed him. According to popular belief, the fire in his laboratory had been brought up from hell and was fueled by demonic substances; therefore, as one might expect, his face was becoming blackened by the smoke.

To summarize the situation, it became a widespread belief that Reverend Arthur Dimmesdale, like many other particularly holy figures throughout the history of Christianity, was being tormented either by Satan himself or by one of Satan's agents disguised as old Roger Chillingworth. This evil representative had been granted divine permission, for a time, to work his way into the minister's personal life and scheme against his soul. No reasonable person, it was acknowledged, could question which side would ultimately prevail. The townspeople watched with unwavering faith, expecting to see their minister emerge from this spiritual battle transformed by the glory he would surely achieve. Yet at the same time, it was heartbreaking to imagine the possibly deadly suffering he would have to endure on his path to victory.

Unfortunately, judging by the darkness and fear visible deep in the troubled minister's eyes, the struggle was intense and the outcome was far from certain.

I notice you've only provided "X." as the heading. This appears to be just a Roman numeral (10) or a placeholder marker rather than a complete heading with descriptive text.

Could you please provide the full heading you'd like me to rewrite? I'd be happy to help make it more contemporary and clear once I can see the complete text.

The Leech and His Patient.

Throughout his entire life, old Roger Chillingworth had possessed a calm disposition, showing kindness despite lacking warm emotions, yet maintaining himself as a pure and honorable man in every aspect of his dealings with the world. He had started his inquiry believing he approached it with the strict and impartial honesty of a judge, seeking nothing but the truth, as though the matter concerned merely abstract lines and shapes of a mathematical equation rather than human emotions and the personal injuries he had suffered. However, as he continued, a dreadful compulsion—a type of intense yet controlled obsession—took hold of the elderly man and refused to release him until he had fulfilled all of its demands. He now probed the unfortunate minister's heart like a prospector digging for gold, or more accurately, like a gravedigger excavating a tomb, perhaps searching for a precious stone buried with the deceased, though more likely to discover only death and decay. What tragedy for his own spirit if this was truly what he was after!

Sometimes, a light flickered in the doctor's eyes, glowing blue and threatening, like the glow from a blazing furnace, or perhaps like one of those flashes of terrifying fire that shot from Bunyan's dreadful entrance in the mountainside, and trembled across the traveler's face. The ground where this shadowy digger was laboring had possibly revealed signs that gave him hope.

"This man," he said to himself during one of these moments, "as pure as people believe him to be—as spiritual as he appears—has inherited a powerful animal nature from either his father or his mother. Let's dig a little deeper in this direction!"

After an extensive search through the minister's shadowy inner world, examining countless valuable elements—his noble hopes for humanity's wellbeing, his deep compassion for souls, his pure thoughts, his natural devotion strengthened through contemplation and study, and enlightened by divine revelation—all of this priceless treasure might have seemed worthless to the one searching for it. Feeling defeated, he would retreat and redirect his investigation elsewhere. He moved with the stealth of a burglar creeping into a room where someone lies in light sleep—or perhaps fully awake—intending to steal the very prize that person protects above all else. Despite his careful planning, the floorboards would occasionally groan under his weight; his clothing would make soft sounds; the presence of his shadow, hovering too close where it shouldn't be, would fall across his target. Put simply, Mr. Dimmesdale, whose sensitive nature often gave him an almost supernatural awareness, would sense in some unclear way that something threatening to his inner calm had entered his sphere. But old Roger Chillingworth possessed his own nearly instinctive understanding; and whenever the minister would suddenly look in his direction with alarm, there sat the doctor—his gentle, attentive, caring, yet never overstepping companion.

Mr. Dimmesdale might have understood this person's true nature more clearly if a certain unhealthy state of mind, which often affects troubled hearts, hadn't made him distrustful of everyone around him. Since he trusted no one as a friend, he couldn't identify his enemy when that person was right in front of him. He continued to maintain a close relationship with him, welcoming the old doctor into his study every day, or visiting the laboratory where, for entertainment, he would observe the processes that transformed common plants into powerful medicines.

One day, resting his forehead against his hand with his elbow propped on the windowsill of the open window that faced the graveyard, he spoke with Roger Chillingworth while the elderly man examined a collection of unattractive plants.

"Where," he asked, glancing sideways at them—for it was the clergyman's peculiarity that he rarely, these days, looked directly at any object, whether human or inanimate—"where, my kind doctor, did you gather those herbs, with such a dark, wilted leaf?"

"Even in the graveyard right here," the physician replied, continuing his work. "These plants are unfamiliar to me. I discovered them growing on a grave that had no headstone or any other marker for the deceased, except for these grotesque weeds that seem to have appointed themselves as his memorial. They sprouted from his heart, and perhaps they represent some terrible secret that was buried along with him—something he would have been better off confessing while he was still alive."

"Perhaps," said Mr. Dimmesdale, "he sincerely wanted it, but couldn't."

"And why?" the physician replied. "Why not; since all the forces of nature call so urgently for the confession of sin, that these black weeds have grown up out of a buried heart, to reveal an unspoken crime?"

"That, good Sir, is nothing more than your imagination," the minister responded. "There can be, if I'm correct in my prediction, no power except Divine mercy that can reveal the secrets buried within a human heart, whether through spoken words, symbols, or signs. The heart that makes itself guilty of such secrets must necessarily keep them hidden until the day when all concealed things will be brought to light. I haven't read or understood Holy Scripture in a way that suggests the revelation of human thoughts and actions on that day is meant to serve as punishment. That would certainly be a superficial understanding of it. No; these revelations, unless I'm greatly mistaken, are simply intended to provide intellectual fulfillment for all thinking beings who will be waiting on that day to see life's dark mysteries finally explained. Understanding people's hearts will be essential to completely solving that mystery. And I believe, furthermore, that hearts containing the wretched secrets you mention will give them up on that final day not reluctantly, but with indescribable joy."

"Then why not reveal them here?" asked Roger Chillingworth, glancing quietly aside at the minister. "Why shouldn't the guilty ones take advantage of this incredible comfort sooner?"

"They usually do," said the minister, gripping his chest tightly as if suffering from a persistent stab of pain. "Many, many troubled souls have confided in me, not just on their deathbeds, but while they were still healthy and had good reputations. And always, after such confessions, oh, what relief I have seen in those sinful people! just like someone who finally breathes fresh air after being suffocated by their own contaminated breath for so long. How could it be any different? Why would a miserable man, guilty of murder, let's say, choose to keep that dead body buried in his own heart, instead of casting it out immediately, and letting the world deal with it!"

"Yet some men bury their secrets this way," observed the calm physician.

"That's true; there are men like that," Mr. Dimmesdale replied. "But, without mentioning more obvious reasons, it's possible that they remain silent because of their very nature. Or—can't we imagine this?—guilty as they might be, they still maintain a passion for God's glory and humanity's well-being, so they avoid revealing themselves as dark and corrupt in people's eyes; because, from that point on, they could accomplish no good; no past wrongs could be made right through better actions. So, in their own indescribable anguish, they move among their fellow human beings, appearing as pure as freshly fallen snow while their hearts are completely marked and stained with wickedness they cannot escape."

"These men are fooling themselves," Roger Chillingworth declared with more intensity than usual, making a small gesture with his index finger. "They're afraid to accept the shame that rightfully belongs to them. Their love for humanity and their devotion to serving God—these sacred impulses may or may not exist alongside the evil forces that their guilt has allowed into their hearts, forces that will inevitably breed a demonic corruption within them. But if they want to honor God, they shouldn't raise their dirty hands toward heaven! If they want to serve their fellow human beings, let them do so by demonstrating the power and reality of conscience by forcing themselves into humble, repentant self-degradation! Are you asking me to believe, my wise and devout friend, that a false appearance can be better—can bring more glory to God or benefit to mankind—than God's own truth? Believe me, such men are only deceiving themselves!"

"That might be true," the young minister said with indifference, dismissing a conversation he felt was pointless or poorly timed. He had developed a natural ability to avoid any subject that disturbed his overly sensitive and anxious nature. "But now, I'd like to ask my skilled doctor whether he truly believes I've benefited from his generous treatment of my frail body?"

Before Roger Chillingworth could respond, they heard the bright, untamed laughter of a young child echoing from the nearby cemetery. Glancing naturally toward the open window—since it was summertime—the minister saw Hester Prynne and little Pearl walking along the path that crossed through the graveyard. Pearl appeared as lovely as the sunshine itself, but she was experiencing one of those stubborn fits of mischief that, whenever they struck her, seemed to place her completely beyond the reach of understanding or human connection. She now hopped disrespectfully from grave to grave; until she reached the wide, flat tombstone bearing a coat of arms that marked the resting place of some distinguished person—possibly Isaac Johnson himself—and she started dancing on top of it. When her mother ordered and pleaded with her to act more properly, little Pearl stopped to collect the spiky seed pods from a tall burdock plant growing next to the grave. Gathering a handful of these burrs, she placed them carefully along the outline of the scarlet letter adorning her mother's chest, where the burrs, true to their nature, clung firmly. Hester made no move to remove them.

Roger Chillingworth had by this time walked up to the window and looked down with a dark, menacing smile.

"There is no law, nor reverence for authority, no regard for human ordinances or opinions, right or wrong, mixed up with that child's composition," he remarked, speaking as much to himself as to his companion. "I saw her, the other day, splash the Governor himself with water, at the cattle-trough in Spring Lane. What, in Heaven's name, is she? Is the imp altogether evil? Does she have affections? Does she have any discoverable principle of being?"

"Nothing, except the freedom that comes from breaking the law," Mr. Dimmesdale replied quietly, as though he had been debating this question in his own mind. "Whether I'm capable of good, I don't know."

The child must have heard their conversation, because she looked up at the window with a bright but mischievous smile full of joy and cleverness, then threw one of the spiky burrs at Reverend Mr. Dimmesdale. The sensitive minister flinched back in nervous fear from the small projectile. When Pearl noticed his reaction, she clapped her tiny hands together in wild delight. Hester Prynne had also instinctively looked up, and all four people, both old and young, stared at each other in complete silence until the child burst into loud laughter and called out, "Come away, mother! Come away, or that old Black Man over there will catch you! He's already gotten hold of the minister. Come away, mother, or he'll catch you too! But he can't catch little Pearl!"

So she led her mother away, jumping, dancing, and moving playfully in wild ways among the burial mounds of the deceased, like a being that shared nothing with a past and buried generation, nor acknowledged any connection to it. It seemed as though she had been created anew from fresh elements, and therefore must naturally be allowed to live her own life and make her own rules, without her unusual behaviors being counted against her as wrongdoing.

"There goes a woman," Roger Chillingworth continued after a pause, "who, whatever her faults may be, doesn't carry that burden of hidden sin which you consider so terrible to bear. Do you think Hester Prynne is any less miserable because of that scarlet letter on her chest?"

"I truly believe that," the clergyman replied. "However, I cannot speak for her. There was an expression of pain on her face that I wish I hadn't had to witness. But still, I think it must be better for someone who is suffering to be free to show their pain, as this poor woman Hester does, than to hide it all away in their heart."

There was another pause, and the doctor started once again to examine and organize the plants he had collected.

"You asked me a little while ago," he said finally, "for my opinion about your health."

"I did," the clergyman replied, "and I would be happy to learn it. Please speak openly, I ask you, whether it concerns life or death."

"Speak freely and plainly then," said the doctor, still tending to his plants but keeping a careful watch on Mr. Dimmesdale. "Your condition is peculiar—not necessarily because of what it is in itself, or how it shows itself outwardly, at least based on the symptoms I've been able to observe. Having looked at you daily, my good sir, and studied the signs in your appearance for months now, I would consider you a man who is seriously ill, perhaps, yet not so ill that a knowledgeable and attentive physician couldn't reasonably hope to heal you. But—I'm not sure what to say—the illness is something I think I understand, yet I don't understand it at all."

"You're speaking in riddles, learned Sir," said the pale minister, glancing sideways out of the window.

"Then, to speak more directly," the physician continued, "and I ask for your forgiveness, Sir—if forgiveness seems necessary—for this required directness in my words. Let me ask—as your friend—as someone responsible, under God's guidance, for your life and physical health—has every aspect of this condition been completely revealed and explained to me?"

"How can you question it?" asked the minister. "Surely, it would be child's play to call in a doctor and then hide the wound!"

"You would tell me, then, that I know everything?" said Roger Chillingworth deliberately, fixing his eye—bright with intense and focused intelligence—on the minister's face. "So be it! But again! The person who sees only the outward and physical illness often knows just half the sickness he's meant to heal. A bodily disease that we view as complete and self-contained may, in the end, be merely a sign of some disorder in the spiritual realm. Please forgive me once more, good Sir, if my words cast any shadow of offense. You, Sir, of all the men I have known, are the one whose body is most closely joined, infused, and united, so to speak, with the spirit of which it serves as the vessel."

"Then I don't need to ask anything more," said the clergyman, rising somewhat quickly from his chair. "You don't deal, I assume, in medicine for the soul!"

"So, an illness," Roger Chillingworth continued, speaking in the same steady tone and ignoring the interruption as he stood up to face the thin, pale-faced minister with his short, dark, and twisted form, "an illness, a painful spot, if we can call it that, in your spirit, immediately shows itself in your physical body. Do you want your doctor to heal your physical ailment? How can this happen unless you first reveal to him the wound or problem in your soul?"

"No!—not to you!—not to an earthly doctor!" cried Mr. Dimmesdale, passionately, turning his eyes, full and bright, with a kind of fierceness, on old Roger Chillingworth. "Not to you! But if it is the soul's disease, then I commit myself to the one Physician of the soul! He, if it stands with his good pleasure, can cure; or he can kill! Let him do with me as, in his justice and wisdom, he shall see fit. But who are you, that meddles in this matter?—that dares thrust himself between the sufferer and his God?"

With a frantic gesture he rushed out of the room.

"It's good that this step has been taken," Roger Chillingworth said to himself, watching the minister leave with a serious smile. "Nothing has been lost. We'll be friends again soon enough. But look at how passion grips this man and carries him beyond his usual self! Just as with one passion, so it is with another! He has done something reckless just now, this devout Master Dimmesdale, driven by the intense passion of his heart!"

The Leech and his Patient

It wasn't difficult to restore the close friendship between the two companions to exactly the same level it had been before. After spending a few hours alone, the young minister realized that his frayed nerves had driven him to an inappropriate outburst of anger, which nothing the doctor had said justified or excused. He was amazed by how violently he had pushed away the kind old man, who had simply been offering the advice it was his responsibility to give, and which the minister himself had specifically requested. Feeling deeply sorry for his behavior, he quickly made the most thorough apologies possible and begged his friend to continue providing the care that, even if it hadn't succeeded in restoring his health, had most likely kept his weak body alive until now. Roger Chillingworth easily agreed and continued his medical treatment of the minister, doing everything he could to help him with complete sincerity, but always leaving the patient's room at the end of each professional visit with a mysterious and confused smile on his lips. This expression couldn't be seen when Mr. Dimmesdale was present, but became clearly visible as the physician walked out the door.

"What an unusual case!" he murmured. "I need to examine this more thoroughly. There's a peculiar connection between mind and body! Even if it's just for the sake of my profession, I must get to the bottom of this!"

Not long after the events just described, Reverend Mr. Dimmesdale fell into a deep, profound sleep at midday, completely without warning, while sitting in his chair with a large old-fashioned book open before him on the table. The book must have been extraordinarily effective at inducing sleep. The minister's deep rest was particularly striking because he was typically someone whose sleep was light, restless, and easily disturbed, like a small bird perched on a branch. However, his spirit had now retreated so far into itself that he didn't move at all in his chair when old Roger Chillingworth entered the room without taking any special care to be quiet. The physician walked directly in front of his patient, placed his hand on his chest, and pushed aside the clothing that had always covered it, even from professional examination.

Then Mr. Dimmesdale shuddered and moved slightly.

After a short pause, the doctor turned away.

But what a wild expression of wonder, joy, and horror crossed his face! What a ghastly rapture seemed too powerful to be shown only through his eyes and facial features, and so it burst forth through his entire grotesque form, revealing itself wildly through the extreme gestures as he flung his arms toward the ceiling and stomped his foot on the floor! If anyone had witnessed old Roger Chillingworth at that moment of ecstasy, they would not have needed to wonder how Satan behaves when a precious human soul is lost to heaven and claimed for his kingdom.

But what set the physician's ecstasy apart from Satan's was the sense of wonder it contained!

Chapter 11: The Interior of a Heart.

After the incident just described, the relationship between the clergyman and the physician, while outwardly unchanged, had truly taken on a different character than it had before. Roger Chillingworth's mind now had a clear enough path laid out before it. This wasn't exactly the route he had originally planned to follow. Though he seemed calm, gentle, and without passion, there was still, we're afraid, a quiet depth of hatred in this unfortunate old man that had been hidden until now but was now active, leading him to envision a more personal revenge than any human had ever inflicted upon an enemy. To become the one trusted friend to whom all the fear, the guilt, the suffering, the useless repentance, and the returning flood of sinful thoughts would be confessed, though expelled in vain! All that guilty grief, concealed from the world whose great heart would have shown pity and forgiveness, would instead be revealed to him, the Merciless, to him, the Unforgiving! All that dark wealth would be poured out upon the very man to whom nothing else could so perfectly repay the debt of revenge!

The minister's timid and delicate nature had prevented this plan from working. Roger Chillingworth, however, felt nearly as satisfied with how things had turned out, which Providence—using both the avenger and his victim for its own ends, and perhaps showing mercy where it appeared to be delivering punishment—had put in place of his evil schemes. A revelation, he could almost claim, had been given to him. It didn't matter much, for his purpose, whether it came from heaven or from some other realm. With its help, in all the future interactions between him and Mr. Dimmesdale, not just the outward appearance, but the deepest soul of the minister seemed to be laid bare before his eyes, so that he could observe and understand its every motion. From that point forward, he became not just an observer, but a main participant in the troubled minister's inner world. He could manipulate him however he wanted. Did he want to torment him with a sharp pain of suffering? The victim was constantly being tortured; it only required knowing which lever controlled the machine—and the physician knew it perfectly! Did he want to shock him with sudden terror? As if at the wave of a sorcerer's wand, a horrible ghost appeared—a thousand ghosts appeared—in countless forms, representing death, or even more terrible disgrace, all gathering around the clergyman, and pointing with their fingers at his chest!

All this was accomplished with such perfect subtlety that the minister, though he constantly felt a vague sense of some evil influence watching over him, could never understand what it actually was. It's true that he looked at the old physician's deformed figure with doubt and fear—sometimes even with horror and bitter hatred. The doctor's gestures, his way of walking, his grizzled beard, his smallest and most casual actions, even the style of his clothes, were disgusting to the clergyman's eyes; this served as a reliable sign of a deeper hatred in the minister's heart than he was willing to admit to himself. Since it was impossible to find a reason for such distrust and disgust, Mr. Dimmesdale, aware that the poison from one diseased spot was contaminating his entire heart, blamed all his bad feelings on this cause alone. He criticized himself for his negative feelings toward Roger Chillingworth, ignored the lesson he should have learned from these feelings, and did his best to eliminate them completely. When he couldn't manage this, he still continued, as a matter of principle, to maintain his friendly social relationship with the old man, constantly giving him opportunities to perfect the purpose to which the avenger had dedicated himself—poor, abandoned creature that he was, and more miserable than his victim.

While suffering from physical illness and being consumed and tormented by some dark anguish of the soul, and surrendered to the schemes of his most deadly enemy, the Reverend Mr. Dimmesdale had gained remarkable popularity in his religious role. He earned this success, in large measure, through his suffering. His mental abilities, his moral insights, his capacity for feeling and expressing emotion, were maintained in a state of extraordinary intensity by the constant pain and torment of his daily existence. His reputation, though still growing, already eclipsed the more restrained standing of his fellow ministers, distinguished as many of them were. Among them were scholars who had devoted more years to mastering complex knowledge related to the religious profession than Mr. Dimmesdale had been alive; and who might reasonably, therefore, be more deeply learned in such substantial and worthwhile achievements than their younger colleague. There were men, as well, of a more robust mental constitution than his, and blessed with a much greater portion of sharp, tough, iron, or granite comprehension; which, properly combined with an adequate measure of theological substance, forms a highly respected, effective, and unlovable type of the ministerial class. There were others, furthermore, genuine saintly fathers, whose abilities had been refined through exhausting labor among their books, and through careful reflection, and purified, additionally, by spiritual communion with the higher realm, into which their moral purity had nearly admitted these sacred figures, with their earthly bodies still attached to them. All that they lacked was the gift that came upon the chosen apostles at Pentecost, in tongues of flame; representing, it would appear, not the ability to speak in foreign and unfamiliar languages, but that of reaching all of humanity in the heart's natural language. These fathers, otherwise so apostolic, lacked Heaven's final and most precious confirmation of their calling, the Tongue of Flame. They would have searched in vain—had they ever imagined searching—to convey the most profound truths through the simplest means of everyday words and images. Their voices reached down, distant and unclear, from the elevated heights where they customarily resided.

Most likely, Mr. Dimmesdale naturally belonged to this latter group of men based on many aspects of his character. He would have climbed to the highest peaks of faith and holiness, if this inclination hadn't been blocked by the weight of whatever crime or suffering it was his fate to bear. This burden kept him down at the same level as the lowest people; him, a man with heavenly qualities, whose voice angels might otherwise have heard and responded to! Yet it was this very burden that gave him such deep understanding of humanity's sinful nature; his heart beat in harmony with theirs, absorbing their pain and sending his own waves of anguish through thousands of other hearts, expressed through bursts of sorrowful, compelling speech. Usually persuasive, but sometimes frightening! The people didn't understand the force that moved them in this way. They considered the young minister a miracle of righteousness. They believed him to be the voice of Heaven's messages of wisdom, correction, and love. In their view, the very earth he walked on was made sacred. The unmarried women in his congregation grew pale in his presence, overcome by a passion so filled with religious feeling that they mistook it for pure devotion, and openly offered it up from their pure hearts as their most precious gift at the altar. The elderly members of his congregation, seeing Mr. Dimmesdale's weak body while they themselves remained strong despite their age, believed he would reach heaven before them, and told their children that their old bones should be buried near their young pastor's sacred grave. And during all this time, perhaps, when poor Mr. Dimmesdale thought about his grave, he wondered whether grass would ever grow on it, since something cursed would be buried there!

The unbearable agony this public worship caused him was beyond description! His true nature drove him to worship truth itself, viewing everything else as mere shadows—completely weightless and worthless unless it contained divine essence as its very core. So what was he then? Something real and substantial, or the faintest shadow of all? He desperately wanted to stand up in his own pulpit, raise his voice to its fullest power, and reveal to his congregation exactly what he really was. "I, the one you see wearing these black robes of ministry—I, who climb into this sacred pulpit and lift my pale face toward heaven, claiming the right to communicate with the Almighty on your behalf—I, whose everyday life you believe reflects the holiness of Enoch—I, whose footsteps you imagine leave a shining path for future pilgrims to follow toward paradise—I, who have baptized your children with my own hands—I, who have spoken final prayers over your dying loved ones while they heard the faint 'Amen' echoing from the world they were leaving behind—I, your minister, whom you respect and trust so deeply, am nothing but complete corruption and deception!"

More than once, Mr. Dimmesdale had entered the pulpit with the intention of never coming down those steps until he had spoken words like those mentioned above. More than once, he had cleared his throat and taken in that long, deep, shaking breath which, when released, would carry the dark secret of his soul. More than once—no, more than a hundred times—he had actually spoken! Spoken! But in what way? He had told his congregation that he was completely corrupt, a more wicked companion than the most wicked, the worst of all sinners, something disgusting, a creature of unthinkable evil; and that the only surprising thing was that they didn't see his miserable body wither away before their very eyes from God's burning anger! Could there be clearer words than these? Wouldn't the people jump up from their seats all at once and drag him down from the pulpit he was contaminating? Not at all! They heard everything and only respected him more. They had no idea what deadly meaning was hidden in those self-condemning words. "The holy young man!" they said to each other. "A saint on earth! If he can see such sinfulness in his own pure soul, what horrible sight would he see in yours or mine!" The minister knew very well—the clever but guilt-ridden fraud that he was!—how his vague confession would be understood. He had tried to deceive himself by admitting to a guilty conscience, but had only gained another sin and a shame he recognized himself, without even the brief comfort of fooling himself. He had spoken the absolute truth and turned it into the biggest lie. And yet, by his very nature, he loved truth and hated lies more than most men ever did. Therefore, above everything else, he hated his wretched self!

His inner turmoil led him to practices that aligned more with the old, corrupt faith of Rome than with the enlightened teachings of the church where he had been raised. In Mr. Dimmesdale's private chamber, locked away from view, he kept a bloody whip.

Many times, this Protestant and Puritan minister had used it on his own shoulders, laughing bitterly at himself all the while, and striking even more mercilessly because of that harsh laughter. He also made it his habit, as many other devout Puritans had done, to fast—though not like them, who fasted to cleanse the body and make it a better vessel for divine enlightenment, but severely, until his knees shook beneath him, as an act of self-punishment. He also kept watch through the night, evening after evening, sometimes in complete darkness, sometimes with a flickering lamp, and sometimes studying his own reflection in a mirror under the brightest light he could cast upon it. This represented the endless self-examination through which he tormented himself, though he could never achieve purification. During these extended nighttime vigils, his mind often became unsteady, and apparitions seemed to drift before him—perhaps glimpsed uncertainly in their own dim glow in the distant shadows of the room, or more clearly and right beside him, within the mirror's surface. Sometimes it was a crowd of demonic figures that sneered and taunted the pale minister, gesturing for him to follow them; other times it was a gathering of radiant angels who ascended heavily, weighed down by sorrow, but became more spiritual as they climbed higher. Sometimes the dead friends of his youth appeared, along with his white-bearded father wearing a saintly scowl, and his mother, who turned her face away as she passed. The ghost of a mother—the faintest illusion of a mother—I think she still might have cast a compassionate look toward her son! And then, through the room that these ghostly thoughts had made so frightening, Hester Prynne glided past, leading little Pearl in her red dress, pointing her finger first at the scarlet letter on her chest, and then at the minister's own heart.

None of these visions ever completely fooled him. At any moment, through sheer willpower, he could see through their hazy lack of reality and remind himself that they weren't solid like the carved oak table over there or that large, square, leather-bound volume of religious texts with its brass clasps. Yet despite this, these visions were, in a way, the most real and meaningful things the troubled minister encountered in his daily life. This is the unbearable tragedy of living such a dishonest existence—it drains the life and meaning from all the genuine things around us, things that Heaven intended to bring joy and nourishment to our spirits. For someone living a lie, the entire world becomes false—it feels unreal, it crumbles to nothing when he tries to grasp it. And he himself, as long as he presents himself falsely, becomes nothing more than a shadow, or really stops existing altogether. The only truth that kept Mr. Dimmesdale anchored to real existence in this world was the torment deep within his soul and the honest way that suffering showed on his face. If he had ever managed to smile and put on a cheerful expression, such a man would never have existed!

On one of those terrible nights, which we have briefly mentioned but avoided describing in detail, the minister suddenly rose from his chair. A new idea had occurred to him. Perhaps it might bring him a moment's peace. Dressing himself as carefully as if he were preparing for public worship, and in exactly the same way, he quietly crept down the staircase, unlocked the door, and stepped outside.

Chapter 12: The Minister's Vigil.

Walking as if in the shadow of a dream, and perhaps actually under the influence of a kind of sleepwalking, Mr. Dimmesdale reached the place where, so long ago now, Hester Prynne had endured her first hours of public shame. The same platform or scaffold, blackened and stained by weather from the storms and sunshine of seven long years, and worn down by the footsteps of many criminals who had climbed it since then, still stood beneath the balcony of the meeting-house. The minister climbed the steps.

It was a dark night in early May. A thick blanket of clouds covered the entire sky from top to bottom. If the same crowd that had watched as witnesses while Hester Prynne endured her punishment could have been called together now, they wouldn't have been able to make out any face above the platform, or even the outline of a human figure, in the dark gray of midnight. But the entire town was asleep. There was no danger of being discovered. The minister could stand there, if he wanted to, until morning light appeared in the east, with no other risk than the damp and cold night air seeping into his body, stiffening his joints with arthritis, and blocking his throat with congestion and coughing; which would prevent tomorrow's expectant congregation from hearing his prayer and sermon. No eye could see him, except for that always-watching one that had seen him in his private room, using the bloody whip. Why, then, had he come here? Was it just a false show of repentance? A false show, indeed, but one in which his soul was playing games with itself! A false show that made angels blush and cry, while demons celebrated with mocking laughter! He had been driven here by the force of that Guilt which followed him everywhere, and whose own sister and closely connected companion was that Fear which always pulled him back, with her shaking grip, just when the other urge had rushed him to the edge of confession. Poor, wretched man! What right did someone as weak as him have to burden himself with crime? Crime is for those with iron nerves, who can choose either to bear it, or, if it becomes too much, to use their fierce and wild strength for a good cause, and throw it off immediately! This weak and most delicate of souls could do neither, yet constantly did one thing or another, which twisted together, in the same impossible knot, the pain of heaven-defying guilt and useless repentance.

Standing on the scaffold during this meaningless display of

atonement, Mr. Dimmesdale was overwhelmed by a terrible mental anguish, as though the entire universe was staring at a scarlet mark on his bare chest, directly over his heart. At that exact location, there truly was, and had been for a long time, the gnawing and toxic bite of physical pain. Unable to control himself or hold back through any act of willpower, he cried out loudly; a scream that echoed through the night, bouncing from house to house and reverberating off the distant hills; as though a group of demons, sensing such profound misery and fear in the sound, had turned it into their toy and were tossing it back and forth among themselves.

"It's finished!" the minister whispered, burying his face in his hands. "The entire town will wake up and rush outside, only to discover me standing here!"

But that wasn't what happened. The scream had probably sounded much louder to his own shocked ears than it really was. The town didn't wake up; or if it did, the sleepy residents thought the cry was either something terrifying from a nightmare, or the sound of witches whose voices, during that time, were frequently heard passing over the settlements or isolated homes as they flew through the air with Satan. The clergyman, therefore, hearing no signs of commotion, uncovered his eyes and looked around. At one of the bedroom windows of Governor Bellingham's mansion, which stood some distance away on another street, he saw the figure of the old magistrate himself, holding a lamp, wearing a white nightcap on his head, and wrapped in a long white robe. He looked like a ghost, summoned at an inappropriate hour from the grave. The cry had clearly startled him. At another window of the same house, old Mistress Hibbins, the Governor's sister, also appeared with a lamp, which, even from that distance, showed the expression on her bitter and unhappy face. She stuck her head out from the window frame and looked nervously upward. Without a doubt, this elderly witch-woman had heard Mr. Dimmesdale's cry, and understood it, with all its countless echoes and reverberations, as the noise of demons and night-witches, with whom she was widely known to venture into the forest.

Spotting the glow from Governor Bellingham's lamp, the elderly woman quickly put out her own light and disappeared. She might have risen up into the clouds. The minister couldn't see what happened to her after that. The magistrate, after carefully watching the darkness—though he could barely see anything more than if he were staring into solid stone—stepped back from the window.

The minister became relatively calm. However, his eyes were soon met by a small, flickering light that was initially far away but was coming closer up the street. The light cast a beam of recognition on various objects: a post here, a garden fence there, a latticed window pane in one spot, a pump with its full water trough in another, and then an arched oak door with an iron knocker and a rough log serving as a doorstep. Reverend Mr. Dimmesdale observed all these tiny details, even while he remained firmly convinced that his fate was creeping closer with each footstep he could now hear, and that the lantern's glow would shine on him within moments, exposing the secret he had kept hidden for so long. As the light came nearer, he saw within its bright circle his fellow clergyman—or more precisely, his professional mentor and deeply cherished friend—Reverend Mr. Wilson, who, as Mr. Dimmesdale now guessed, had been offering prayers at the bedside of someone dying. And indeed he had. The kind old minister was coming directly from the death chamber of Governor Winthrop, who had departed from earth to heaven within that very hour. And now, encircled like the holy figures of ancient times with a brilliant halo that made him shine in this dark night of sin—as though the deceased Governor had bequeathed him a portion of his glory, or as though he had absorbed some of the distant radiance of the heavenly city while gazing toward it to watch the victorious pilgrim enter through its gates—now, in essence, good Father Wilson was walking home, using a lit lantern to guide his steps! The glow of this light sparked these imaginative thoughts in Mr. Dimmesdale, who smiled—indeed, nearly laughed at them—and then wondered whether he was losing his mind.

As Reverend Wilson walked past the scaffold, wrapping his Geneva cloak tightly around himself with one arm while holding the lantern against his chest with the other, the minister could barely stop himself from calling out.

"Good evening to you, respected Father Wilson! Please come up here, I ask you, and spend a pleasant hour with me!"

Good heavens! Had Mr. Dimmesdale actually spoken out loud? For a moment, he thought those words had come from his mouth. But he had only said them in his mind. The respected Father Wilson kept walking slowly forward, watching the muddy path carefully as he went, never once looking toward the platform where guilt stood. When the flickering lantern light disappeared completely, the minister realized from the weakness that washed over him that those last few moments had been filled with overwhelming fear and stress. His mind had tried to cope with the tension by creating a kind of dark, twisted sense of humor.

Shortly afterward, the same dark sense of irony crept back among the serious thoughts in his mind. He felt his body growing rigid from the unusual cold of the night, and wondered if he would even be able to walk down the scaffold steps. Dawn would arrive and discover him there. The neighborhood would start to wake up. The first person to rise, stepping outside in the faint early light, would notice a shadowy figure standing high on the platform of public disgrace; and, driven half mad by both fear and curiosity, would go knocking from house to house, calling everyone to come see what they would surely believe was the ghost of some dead criminal. A confused commotion would spread like wings from one home to the next. Then—as the morning light grew brighter—elderly community leaders would hurry outside in their nightgowns, along with respectable women who hadn't bothered to change out of their sleepwear. The entire group of proper citizens, who had never before been seen with even a single hair out of place, would appear in public looking as disheveled as if they were trapped in a bad dream. Old Governor Bellingham would emerge with a stern expression, his elaborate Jacobean collar crooked and twisted; and Mistress Hibbins would appear with forest twigs still caught in her dress, looking more bitter than usual after getting barely any sleep following her nighttime journey; and good Father Wilson too, after spending half the night beside a dying person's bed, would be irritated at being woken so early from his dreams of heavenly saints. The church elders and deacons from Mr. Dimmesdale's congregation would also rush over, along with the young unmarried women who worshipped their minister so completely that they had created a sacred place for him in their pure hearts; these women, in their haste and panic, would barely have taken time to properly cover themselves with their head scarves. Everyone, in short, would come stumbling out of their homes, turning their shocked and terrified faces toward the scaffold. Who would they see standing there, with the red light of sunrise on his forehead? Who else but the Reverend Arthur Dimmesdale, nearly frozen to death, crushed by shame, and standing exactly where Hester Prynne had once stood!

Swept up by the bizarre and horrifying nature of this scene, the minister unconsciously and to his own tremendous shock broke into loud laughter. A light, carefree, childlike laugh immediately answered him, and in those sounds—with his heart racing, though he couldn't tell if it was from intense pain or equally sharp pleasure—he recognized little Pearl's voice.

"Pearl! Little Pearl!" he called out after pausing for a moment; then, lowering his voice, he said, "Hester! Hester Prynne! Are you there?"

"Yes; it is Hester Prynne!" she replied, sounding surprised; and the minister heard her footsteps coming closer from the sidewalk where she had been walking. "It is I, and my little Pearl."

"Where do you come from, Hester?" the minister asked. "What brought you here?"

"I've been keeping watch at a deathbed," Hester Prynne replied. "I was at Governor Winthrop's deathbed, where I took his measurements for a burial robe, and now I'm heading home to my house."

"Come up here, Hester, you and little Pearl," said Reverend Mr. Dimmesdale. "You have both been here before, but I was not with you. Come up here once again, and we will stand all three together!"

She quietly climbed the steps and stood on the platform, holding little Pearl's hand. The minister reached for the child's other hand and grasped it. The instant he did, what felt like a powerful surge of new life—life different from his own—flooded into his heart like a rushing river and raced through all his veins, as though the mother and child were sharing their living warmth with his nearly lifeless body. The three of them created an electric connection.

"Minister!" whispered little Pearl.

"What would you say, child?" asked Mr. Dimmesdale.

"Will you stand here with mother and me tomorrow at noon?" asked Pearl.

"No, not so, my little Pearl," the minister replied; for with the fresh energy of the moment, all the fear of public exposure that had been the torment of his life for so long had come back to him, and he was already shaking at the situation in which—with an odd joy, nonetheless—he now found himself. "Not so, my child. I will, indeed, stand with your mother and you on another day, but not tomorrow."

Pearl laughed and tried to pull her hand away. But the minister held it firmly.

"Just one more moment, my child!" he said.

"But will you promise," asked Pearl, "to take my hand, and mother's hand, tomorrow at noon?"

"Not now, Pearl," said the minister, "but another time."

"And what other time?" the child persisted.

"On the great judgment day," the minister whispered—and, strangely enough, his awareness that he was a professional teacher of the truth compelled him to respond to the child in this way. "Then, and there, before the judgment seat, your mother, and you, and I must stand together. But the daylight of this world will not witness our meeting!"

Pearl laughed again.

They stood in the midday light of that extraordinary brilliance.

But before Mr. Dimmesdale had finished speaking, a bright light spread far and wide across the cloudy sky. It was undoubtedly caused by one of those meteors that night watchers often see burning out in the empty regions of the atmosphere. The light was so powerful that it completely lit up the thick layer of clouds between the sky and earth. The great dome of the sky brightened like an enormous lamp. It revealed the familiar street scene with the clarity of midday, but also with the awe that unfamiliar light always brings to familiar objects. The wooden houses with their overhanging upper floors and charming peaked roofs; the doorsteps and entryways with early grass growing around them; the garden plots, dark with freshly turned soil; the wheel tracks, barely worn, and even in the marketplace, bordered with green on both sides—everything was visible, but with such a strange quality that seemed to give the things of this world a different moral meaning than they had ever carried before. And there stood the minister with his hand over his heart; and Hester Prynne with the embroidered letter shining on her chest; and little Pearl, herself a symbol and the connecting link between those two. They stood in the brightness of that strange and solemn light, as if it were the illumination that would reveal all secrets and the dawn that would unite all who belong to one another.

There was something magical and mischievous in little Pearl's eyes, and her face, as she looked up at the minister, displayed that playful smile that often gave her such an impish expression. She pulled her hand away from Mr. Dimmesdale's and pointed across the street. But he pressed both his hands against his chest and lifted his gaze toward the sky above.

Nothing was more common in those days than to interpret all meteoric appearances and other natural phenomena that occurred with less regularity than the rising and setting of the sun and moon as revelations from a supernatural source. A blazing spear, a sword of flame, a bow, or a bundle of arrows seen in the midnight sky foretold Indian warfare. Disease was known to have been predicted by a shower of crimson light. We question whether any significant event, whether good or bad, ever happened to New England from its settlement through Revolutionary times without the inhabitants having been previously warned by some spectacle of this kind. Sometimes, crowds had witnessed it. More often, however, its believability depended on the testimony of some solitary eyewitness who saw the wonder through the colored, magnifying, and distorting lens of his imagination and shaped it more clearly in his later reflection. It was indeed a magnificent idea that the destiny of nations should be revealed in these awesome hieroglyphics across the dome of heaven. Such a wide scroll might not be considered too vast for Providence to write a people's fate upon. This belief was favored by our ancestors, as it suggested that their young commonwealth was under celestial protection of particular closeness and severity. But what should we say when an individual discovers a revelation addressed to himself alone on the same enormous sheet of record! In such a case, it could only be the sign of a severely disturbed mental condition, when a man, made unhealthily self-absorbed by long, intense, and secret suffering, had spread his self-centeredness over the entire expanse of nature, until the sky itself would seem nothing more than a suitable page for his soul's history and destiny!

We attribute it, therefore, entirely to the sickness in his own vision and soul, that the minister, gazing upward toward the highest point in the sky, saw there the form of an enormous letter—the letter A—outlined in streaks of dim red light. It's not that the meteor couldn't have appeared at that spot, glowing faintly through a curtain of clouds; but it wouldn't have had the shape that his guilty mind assigned to it; or, at the very least, it would have been so unclear that someone else's guilt might have recognized a completely different symbol in it.

There was a strange detail that marked Mr. Dimmesdale's mental state at that moment. While he stared upward at the sky above, he remained completely conscious that little Pearl was pointing her finger toward old Roger Chillingworth, who stood not far from the scaffold. The minister seemed to see him with the same look that spotted the miraculous letter. The meteor's light gave his face, like everything else, a new look; or perhaps the physician wasn't being careful then, as he always was at other times, to conceal the hatred with which he stared at his victim. Surely, if the meteor lit up the sky and revealed the earth with a terror that warned Hester Prynne and the clergyman of judgment day, then Roger Chillingworth could have been mistaken for the devil himself, standing there with both a smile and a frown, ready to claim what belonged to him. The expression was so clear, or the minister saw it so sharply, that it seemed to stay burned into the darkness even after the meteor disappeared, creating an effect as if the street and everything else had suddenly been wiped out.

"Who is that man, Hester?" gasped Mr. Dimmesdale, overwhelmed with terror. "He makes me shiver! Do you know the man? I hate him, Hester!"

She remembered her oath, and remained silent.

"I'm telling you, my soul trembles at the sight of him!" the minister muttered once more. "Who is he? Who is he? Can't you do anything to help me? I feel a terrible, indescribable fear of that man!"

"Minister," said little Pearl, "I can tell you who he is!"

"Hurry, then, child!" said the minister, leaning his ear close to her lips. "Hurry!—and speak as quietly as you can whisper."

Pearl whispered something in his ear that did sound like human speech, but it was really just the kind of nonsense that children can be heard entertaining themselves with for hours at a time. In any case, if it contained any secret information about old Roger Chillingworth, it was in a language the learned minister didn't understand, and it only added to his confusion. The mischievous child then burst out laughing.

"Are you mocking me now?" said the minister.

"You weren't brave! You weren't honest!" the child answered. "You wouldn't promise to take my hand and mother's hand tomorrow at noon!"

"Respected Sir," replied the doctor, who had now stepped forward to the base of the platform. "Devout Master Dimmesdale, is this really you? My goodness, indeed! We scholars, whose minds are buried in our books, need to be carefully watched over! We daydream while we're awake, and sleepwalk through our lives. Come, good Sir, and my dear friend, please, let me take you home!"

"How did you know I was here?" asked the minister, fearfully.

"Truly, and in good faith," answered Roger Chillingworth, "I knew nothing about it. I had spent most of the night at the bedside of the honorable Governor Winthrop, doing whatever my limited skill could do to comfort him. As he was going home to a better world, I was also on my way home when this strange light appeared. Come with me, I beg you, Reverend Sir; otherwise you will be poorly prepared to perform your Sabbath duties tomorrow. Ah! Look now, how they trouble the mind—these books!—these books! You should study less, good Sir, and enjoy a little recreation; or these nighttime fantasies will take hold of you."

"I will go home with you," said Mr. Dimmesdale.

With a cold sense of despair, like someone waking up completely drained from a terrible nightmare, he surrendered himself to the doctor and was taken away.

The following day, however, being the Sabbath, he delivered a sermon that was considered the most profound and powerful, and the most filled with divine inspiration, that had ever come from his mouth. Many souls, it is said, were led to the truth through the power of that sermon, and promised themselves to maintain a sacred gratitude toward Mr. Dimmesdale for all the years to come. But as he descended the pulpit steps, the gray-bearded sexton approached him, holding up a black glove that the minister recognized as his own.

"It was discovered," the sexton explained, "this morning on the platform where criminals are displayed for public humiliation. I believe Satan left it there, planning a mocking joke aimed at your reverence. But truly, he was shortsighted and stupid, as he always has been and always will be. An innocent hand doesn't need a glove to hide it!"

"Thank you, my good friend," the minister said seriously, though his heart was startled; his memory was so muddled that he had nearly convinced himself the events of the previous night were just a dream. "Yes, it does appear to be my glove!"

"And since Satan decided to steal it, your reverence will have to deal with him harshly from now on," commented the old sexton with a grim smile. "But did your reverence hear about the supernatural sign that was witnessed last night?—a large red letter in the sky,—the letter A, which we believe represents Angel. Since our good Governor Winthrop became an angel last night, it was surely appropriate that there should be some announcement of it!"

"No," the minister replied, "I hadn't heard about it."

Chapter 13: Another View of Hester.

During her final private meeting with Mr. Dimmesdale, Hester Prynne was stunned by the deteriorated state she discovered the minister in. His composure appeared completely shattered. His moral strength had crumbled into something weaker than a child's frailty. It lay powerless and defeated, even though his mental abilities maintained their original vigor, or had possibly gained an unhealthy intensity that only illness could have produced. With her understanding of a series of events concealed from everyone else, she could easily conclude that, beyond the natural workings of his own guilt, a dreadful force had been applied, and continued to work against Mr. Dimmesdale's peace and well-being. Knowing what this unfortunate, broken man had once been, her entire spirit was stirred by the trembling fear with which he had reached out to her—the rejected woman—for protection against his instinctively recognized adversary. She determined, furthermore, that he deserved her complete assistance. Having little experience, during her long isolation from society, in judging her sense of right and wrong by any external measure, Hester recognized—or appeared to recognize—that she bore a duty toward the clergyman that she owed to no one else, nor to the entire world beyond. The connections that bound her to the rest of humanity—bonds of flowers, or silk, or gold, or whatever their substance—had all been severed. Here existed the unbreakable chain of shared transgression, which neither he nor she could destroy. Like every other bond, it carried with it certain duties.

Hester Prynne no longer held exactly the same position that we saw her in during the early days of her public shame. Years had passed. Pearl was now seven years old. Her mother, wearing the scarlet letter on her chest that sparkled with its elaborate embroidery, had become a familiar sight to the townspeople. As often happens when someone stands out prominently in the community while not interfering with either public or private interests and convenience, a kind of general respect had eventually developed toward Hester Prynne. It speaks well of human nature that, except when selfishness comes into play, people are more inclined to love than to hate. Hatred, through a gradual and quiet process, can even transform into love, unless this change is blocked by constantly renewed irritation of the original hostile feelings. In Hester Prynne's case, there was neither irritation nor annoyance. She never fought against the public but accepted its worst treatment without complaint; she made no demands for compensation for what she had endured; she did not burden their sympathies. Furthermore, the spotless purity of her life during all these years when she had been marked for disgrace worked greatly in her favor. With nothing left to lose in the eyes of society, and with no hope and apparently no desire to gain anything, it could only be genuine respect for virtue that had brought the poor outcast back to righteous ways.

Hester in the House of Mourning

People noticed that while Hester never claimed even the smallest right to participate in society's privileges—asking for nothing more than to breathe the same air as everyone else and earn daily bread for little Pearl and herself through honest work—she was always ready to acknowledge her connection to humanity whenever there was good to be done. No one was more willing than she to give from her meager resources to anyone in need; this remained true even when bitter-hearted beggars would respond with insults to the food she regularly brought to their doors, or to the clothing made by hands skilled enough to have embroidered a king's robes. No one was more selfless than Hester when disease swept through the town. During every disaster, whether it affected the whole community or just individuals, this outcast from society immediately found her place. She entered homes darkened by trouble not as a visitor, but as someone who belonged there; as if that gloomy atmosphere was the natural setting for her to connect with other people. The embroidered letter glowed there, bringing comfort through its otherworldly light. While everywhere else it represented sin, in sickrooms it became a guiding candle. It had even cast its glow during a sufferer's final moments, reaching across the boundary between life and death. It had shown dying people where to place their trust, when earthly light was fading and the light of the afterlife had not yet reached them. In these critical moments, Hester's true nature emerged as warm and generous; she was a wellspring of human compassion, never failing to meet any genuine need, and never exhausted no matter how great the demand. Her chest, marked with its badge of shame, became only a softer pillow for any head that needed rest. She had appointed herself as a Sister of Mercy; or perhaps we should say that the world's harsh treatment had appointed her to this role, when neither the world nor she had foreseen this outcome. The letter had become the symbol of her mission. She proved so helpful—with such power to act and to understand others' pain—that many people refused to interpret the scarlet A according to its original meaning. They said it stood for Able; such was Hester Prynne's strength, the unique strength of a woman.

Only the darkened house could hold her. When sunlight returned, she was nowhere to be found. Her shadow had vanished from the doorway. The caring helper had left without a single look back to collect any gratitude that might exist in the hearts of those she had served so devotedly. When she encountered them on the street, she never lifted her head to acknowledge their greetings. If they insisted on approaching her, she would place her finger on the scarlet letter and continue walking. This behavior might have been pride, but it resembled humility so closely that it created all the gentle effects of that virtue on the public's perception. The public has a tyrannical nature; it can refuse basic fairness when it's demanded too forcefully as an entitlement; but just as often it grants more than fairness when the request is made in the way tyrants prefer—appealing entirely to their generosity. Understanding Hester Prynne's behavior as this type of appeal, society began to regard its former victim with a kinder expression than she wished to receive, or perhaps than she had earned.

The community's rulers, along with its wise and educated citizens, took much longer than ordinary people to recognize Hester's positive qualities. The biases they held in common with everyone else were strengthened within them by a rigid structure of logic, making these prejudices much harder to overcome. Day after day, however, their harsh and inflexible expressions gradually softened into something that, given enough time, might eventually become almost kind. This was the case with men of high standing, whose prominent positions made them responsible for protecting public morality. Meanwhile, ordinary citizens had completely forgiven Hester Prynne for her moral failing; in fact, they had started to view the scarlet letter not as a symbol of that single sin for which she had endured such a long and miserable punishment, but as a sign of her many charitable acts since then. "Do you see that woman wearing the embroidered symbol?" they would tell visitors. "That's our Hester—the town's very own Hester, who shows such kindness to the poor, offers so much help to the sick, and brings such comfort to those who suffer!" Then, it's true, the human tendency to reveal the very worst about ourselves when we see it reflected in someone else would force them to whisper about the dark scandal from years past. Nevertheless, it remained true that in the eyes of these very same people who spoke this way, the scarlet letter had the same effect as a cross on a nun's chest. It gave the person wearing it a kind of sacred quality that allowed her to move safely through any danger. If she had encountered thieves, it would have protected her. Many people reported and believed that a Native American had aimed his arrow at the badge, and that while the arrow hit its target, it fell harmlessly to the ground.

The impact of the symbol—or more precisely, the social position it represented—on Hester Prynne's mind was both profound and strange. All the brightness and delicate beauty of her personality had been burned away by this searing mark, withering and falling off long ago, leaving behind only a stark and severe outline that might have been off-putting if she had possessed friends or companions who could be disturbed by it. Even her physical attractiveness had undergone a comparable transformation. This change might have been partially due to the deliberate plainness of her clothing, and partially due to the absence of warmth in her behavior. It was also a sorrowful change that her abundant and beautiful hair had either been cut away, or was so thoroughly concealed beneath a cap that not a single gleaming strand ever caught the sunlight. While all these factors contributed to the transformation, something deeper was at work—there no longer seemed to be anything in Hester's face that Love could inhabit; nothing in Hester's figure, despite its dignity and sculptural quality, that Passion would ever consider embracing; nothing in Hester's heart that could serve again as a resting place for Affection. Some essential quality had left her, something whose presence had been vital to maintaining her womanhood. This is often the destiny, and such is the harsh evolution, of feminine character and appearance when a woman has faced and endured an experience of extraordinary harshness. If she is entirely gentle, she will perish. If she survives, that gentleness will either be destroyed within her, or—and the external appearance remains the same—buried so far into her soul that it can never emerge again. The second possibility is perhaps the more accurate explanation. A woman who was once truly feminine, and has ceased to be so, might at any time reclaim her womanhood if only the right touch could bring about such a transformation. We shall discover whether Hester Prynne was ever afterward touched in this way, and thus transformed.

Much of the marble-like coldness in Hester's demeanor could be traced to the fact that her life had shifted dramatically from passion and emotion to deep contemplation. Standing isolated in the world—alone in terms of any reliance on society, with only little Pearl to guide and protect—alone and without hope of restoring her social standing, even though she wouldn't have considered such restoration worthwhile anyway—she threw away the remnants of her broken bonds. Society's laws held no authority over her mind. This was an era when human intellect, recently freed from constraints, had become more active and far-reaching than it had been for many centuries. Warriors had toppled nobles and monarchs. Men even bolder than these had dismantled and reorganized—not in reality, but within the realm of ideas, which was their truest domain—the entire framework of old prejudices, along with much of the ancient principles connected to them. Hester Prynne absorbed this revolutionary spirit. She embraced a freedom of intellectual exploration that was common enough across the Atlantic, but which our ancestors, had they been aware of it, would have considered a more deadly sin than the one marked by the scarlet letter. In her isolated cottage by the seashore, thoughts came to her that wouldn't dare enter any other home in New England—shadowy visitors that would have been as dangerous as devils to anyone who entertained them, if they could have been seen even approaching her door.

It's striking how people who think most daringly often follow society's external rules with complete calm. The thinking alone satisfies them, without needing to turn their ideas into real action. This appeared to be true for Hester. However, if little Pearl had never come to her from the spiritual realm, things might have been very different. Hester could have gone down in history alongside

Ann Hutchinson as the founder of a religious movement. During one period of her life, she might have become a prophetess. She might have, and quite possibly would have, been executed by the harsh courts of that time for trying to destroy the foundations of Puritan society. But in raising her child, the mother's passionate ideas found something to focus on. Providence, through this little girl, had given Hester the responsibility of nurturing the beginning and flowering of womanhood, to be cared for and guided through countless challenges. Everything worked against her. The world showed hostility. The child's own character contained something flawed, which constantly suggested she had been born under unfortunate circumstances—the result of her mother's forbidden passion—and frequently caused Hester to wonder, with a bitter heart, whether it was a blessing or a curse that the poor little creature had been born at all.

Indeed, the same troubling question frequently entered her thoughts, concerning all womankind. Was life worth living, even for the most fortunate among them? Regarding her own personal existence, she had long since reached a negative conclusion and considered the matter resolved. A inclination toward deep thinking, while it may keep a woman calm just as it does a man, nevertheless fills her with sorrow. She perceives, perhaps, such a hopeless challenge ahead of her. As an initial step, the entire structure of society must be dismantled and reconstructed from the ground up. Then, the fundamental nature of the opposite sex, or its deeply ingrained hereditary patterns that have become second nature, must be fundamentally altered before woman can be permitted to claim what appears to be a fair and appropriate place. Finally, even with all other obstacles removed, woman cannot benefit from these foundational changes until she herself undergoes an even more profound transformation; during which, possibly, the spiritual essence that contains her deepest truth will be discovered to have disappeared. A woman never resolves these challenges through any amount of reasoning. They cannot be solved, or can only be solved in one manner. If her heart happens to take precedence, these problems disappear. Therefore, Hester Prynne, whose heart had lost its steady and natural rhythm, roamed without guidance through the dark maze of her thoughts; sometimes blocked by an impossible barrier; sometimes retreating from a bottomless abyss. Wild and frightening landscapes surrounded her everywhere, with no place of refuge or peace to be found. Occasionally, a terrible uncertainty tried to overtake her spirit, questioning whether it might not be better to send Pearl immediately to heaven and accept whatever fate Eternal Justice would determine for herself.

The scarlet letter had not accomplished its purpose.

Now, however, her conversation with the Reverend Mr. Dimmesdale on the night of his vigil had given her something new to think about, and showed her a goal that seemed worth any effort and sacrifice to achieve. She had seen the terrible suffering that tormented the minister, or more precisely, that he had stopped fighting against. She could see that he was on the edge of madness, if he hadn't already crossed that line. There was no doubt that while the secret pain of guilt might have some agonizing power, a more deadly poison had been mixed into it by the very person who offered to help. A hidden enemy had constantly stayed by his side, pretending to be a friend and helper, and had used every opportunity this gave him to manipulate the sensitive aspects of Mr. Dimmesdale's character. Hester couldn't help but wonder whether she herself had originally lacked honesty, courage, and faithfulness by allowing the minister to be put in a situation where so much harm could be expected and nothing good could be hoped for. Her only excuse was that she hadn't been able to see any way to save him from a worse destruction than what had already ruined her, except by going along with Roger Chillingworth's plan of disguise. Acting on that feeling, she had made her decision and had chosen what now seemed to be the more miserable option of the two. She decided to make up for her mistake, as much as might still be possible. Made stronger by years of difficult and serious hardship, she no longer felt as unable to deal with Roger Chillingworth as she had on that night when, humiliated by sin and half-crazy from the shame that was still fresh, they had spoken together in the prison cell. She had worked her way up to a higher position since then. The old man, on the other hand, had brought himself closer to her level, or perhaps even lower, through the revenge he had lowered himself to pursue.

Finally, Hester Prynne decided to confront her former husband and do whatever she could to save the victim he had so clearly targeted. She didn't have to wait long for an opportunity. One afternoon, while walking with Pearl in a secluded area of the peninsula, she spotted the old doctor carrying a basket on one arm and a walking stick in the other hand, bent over as he searched the ground for roots and herbs to make his medicines.

Chapter 14: Hester And the Physician.

Hester told little Pearl to run down to the water's edge and play with the shells and tangled seaweed while she spoke with the herb gatherer over there. The child darted away like a bird, and after taking off her shoes to bare her small white feet, she went pattering along the wet shoreline. Every so often she would stop completely and peer curiously into a tidal pool that the receding tide had left behind, creating a mirror for Pearl to see her reflection. Looking back at her from the pool, with dark, shining curls framing her head and a mischievous smile in her eyes, was the image of a little girl whom Pearl, having no other companion to play with, invited to take her hand and race with her. But the imaginary little girl also beckoned back, as if saying, "This is a better place! Come into the pool with me!" And when Pearl stepped in up to her calves, she could see her own white feet at the bottom, while from an even deeper level came the glimmer of what looked like pieces of a smile, drifting back and forth in the rippling water.

Meanwhile, her mother had approached the doctor.

"I need to have a word with you," she said. "Something that's very important to both of us."

"Ah! So it's Mistress Hester who has something to say to old Roger Chillingworth?" he replied, straightening up from his bent position. "With all my heart! Why, Mistress, I hear wonderful news about you from everyone! Just yesterday evening, a magistrate, a wise and godly man, was discussing your situation, Mistress Hester, and told me quietly that there had been discussion about you in the council. They debated whether or not, for the safety of the public good, that scarlet letter could be removed from your chest. I swear on my life, Hester, I pleaded with the honorable magistrate that it should be done immediately!"

"The magistrates don't have the authority to remove this badge," Hester replied calmly. "If I were worthy of being freed from it, it would fall away on its own, or change into something that would convey a different meaning."

"No, then, wear it, if it suits you better," he replied. "A woman must follow her own preferences when it comes to adorning herself. The letter is beautifully embroidered, and looks quite striking on your chest!"

All this time, Hester had been staring steadily at the old man, and she was shocked and amazed to see what a dramatic change had taken place in him over the past seven years. It wasn't so much that he had aged; although signs of getting older were evident, he carried his years well and seemed to maintain a lean strength and sharpness. However, his former appearance as an intellectual and scholarly man, calm and peaceful, which was how she best remembered him, had completely disappeared and been replaced by an eager, probing, almost savage, yet carefully controlled expression. He seemed to want and intend to hide this look behind a smile; but the smile betrayed him, flickering across his face so mockingly that observers could see his darkness even more clearly because of it. From time to time, a flash of red light would also appear in his eyes; as if the old man's soul was burning, continuing to smolder dimly within his chest, until some random surge of emotion would fan it into a brief flame. He suppressed this as quickly as he could, and tried to appear as if nothing like that had occurred.

In short, old Roger Chillingworth served as compelling proof of humanity's ability to transform into a devil, provided one is willing to carry out the devil's work for a sufficient period. This miserable man had accomplished such a transformation by dedicating himself for seven years to the relentless examination of a heart filled with agony, drawing his pleasure from this pursuit, and feeding the blazing torments that he studied and savored.

The scarlet letter blazed on Hester Prynne's chest. Here stood another destroyed life, and she bore some responsibility for this devastation.

"What do you see in my face," the physician asked, "that makes you stare at it so intently?"

"Something that would make me cry, if there were tears bitter enough for it," she replied. "But let's move on! It's about that wretched man over there that I want to talk."

"And what about him?" Roger Chillingworth exclaimed eagerly, as if he relished the subject and was pleased to have a chance to discuss it with the only person he could confide in. "To be honest, Mistress Hester, my thoughts are occupied with that gentleman right now. So speak openly, and I'll respond."

"When we last spoke together," said Hester, "seven years ago now, you chose to force me to promise secrecy about the former relationship between you and me. Since that man's life and reputation were in your hands, I felt I had no choice but to remain silent, just as you demanded. Yet I bound myself to this promise with serious doubts, because having abandoned all obligations to other people, I still had a duty toward him; and something told me I was betraying that duty by agreeing to keep your secret. Since that day, no one has been closer to him than you. You follow his every step. You stay by his side, asleep and awake. You probe his thoughts. You dig into his heart and fester there! You have a grip on his life, and you make him suffer a living death every day; yet he still doesn't know who you are. By allowing this to happen, I have certainly been false to the only man I still had the power to be true to!"

"What choice did you have?" asked Roger Chillingworth. "If I had pointed my finger at this man, it would have thrown him from his pulpit into a prison cell—and from there, perhaps, to the gallows!"

"It would have been better that way!" said Hester Prynne.

"What harm have I caused this man?" Roger Chillingworth asked once more. "I'm telling you, Hester Prynne, the most expensive payment any doctor ever received from a king couldn't have purchased the kind of care I've given to this wretched minister! Without my help, his life would have been consumed by suffering within the first two years after he committed his sin along with you. You see, Hester, his soul didn't have the strength to endure what yours has endured while carrying a burden like your scarlet letter. Oh, I could share an incredible secret! But that's enough! Every medical skill available, I've used on him. The fact that he's still alive today and walking around on this earth is entirely because of me!"

"It would have been better if he had died immediately!" said Hester Prynne.

"Yes, woman, you speak the truth!" cried old Roger Chillingworth, letting the fierce fire of his heart blaze out before her eyes. "It would have been better if he had died at once! No mortal has ever suffered what this man has endured. And all of it, all of it, in the sight of his worst enemy! He has been aware of me. He has felt an influence constantly dwelling upon him like a curse. He knew, through some spiritual sense—for the Creator never made another being so sensitive as this—he knew that no friendly hand was pulling at his heartstrings, and that an eye was looking curiously into him, seeking only evil, and finding it. But he didn't know that the eye and hand were mine! With the superstition common to his brotherhood, he imagined himself given over to a fiend, to be tortured with frightful dreams, and desperate thoughts, the sting of remorse, and despair of pardon; as a foretaste of what awaits him beyond the grave. But it was the constant shadow of my presence!—the closest proximity of the man whom he had most vilely wronged!—and who had grown to exist only through this perpetual poison of the most terrible revenge! Yes, indeed!—he was not mistaken!—there was a fiend at his elbow! A mortal man, with once a human heart, has become a fiend for his special torment!"

The unfortunate doctor, as he spoke these words, raised his hands with an expression of horror, as though he had seen some terrifying figure that he couldn't identify taking the place of his own reflection in a mirror. This was one of those moments—which sometimes happen only after years have passed—when a person's true moral character is honestly revealed to their inner vision. Most likely, he had never seen himself as clearly as he did in that instant.

"Haven't you tortured him enough?" said Hester, noticing the old man's look. "Hasn't he paid you everything?"

"No!—no!—He has only made the debt bigger!" the physician replied; and as he continued speaking, his manner lost its more intense qualities and settled into darkness. "Do you remember me, Hester, as I was nine years ago? Even then, I was in the autumn of my life, and it wasn't early autumn either. But my entire life had been made up of serious, scholarly, thoughtful, quiet years, devoted faithfully to increasing my own knowledge, and faithfully too, though this second goal was only secondary to the first—faithfully devoted to advancing human welfare. No life had been more peaceful and innocent than mine; few lives were so rich with good deeds performed. Do you remember me? Wasn't I, though you might have thought me cold, still a man who was considerate of others, wanting little for himself—kind, honest, fair, and possessing steady, if not passionate feelings? Wasn't I all of this?"

"All this, and more," said Hester.

"And what am I now?" he demanded, looking into her face and allowing all the evil within him to show on his features. "I have already told you what I am! A devil! Who made me this way?"

"It was me!" cried Hester, trembling. "It was me, just as much as him. Why haven't you taken revenge on me?"

"I have left you to the scarlet letter," replied Roger Chillingworth. "If that has not avenged me, I can do nothing more!"

He placed his finger on it, smiling.

"It has avenged you!" answered Hester Prynne.

"I thought as much," said the physician. "And now, what do you want from me regarding this man?"

"I have to tell him the truth," Hester replied with determination. "He needs to see you for who you really are. I don't know what will happen, but I've owed him this honesty for far too long—I've been the cause of his destruction and downfall, and it's time to finally pay that debt. His reputation, his position in this world, and maybe even his life are now in your hands. And I—someone whom the scarlet letter has taught to face the truth, even when that truth burns like red-hot iron piercing the soul—I don't see any benefit in him continuing to live this hollow, ghostly existence, so I won't lower myself to beg for your mercy. Do whatever you want with him! There's nothing good left for him, nothing good for me, nothing good for you! There's nothing good for little Pearl either! There's no way out of this terrible trap we're all caught in!"

"Woman, I could almost pity you!" said Roger Chillingworth, unable to restrain a thrill of admiration as well; for there was a quality almost majestic in the despair which she expressed. "You had great elements. Perhaps, if you had met earlier with a better love than mine, this evil would not have been. I pity you, for the good that has been wasted in your nature!"

"And I pity you," Hester Prynne replied, "for the hatred that has turned a wise and just man into a demon! Will you cleanse it from yourself and become human again? If not for his sake, then twice as much for your own! Forgive him, and leave his punishment to the Power that rightfully claims it! I just said that nothing good could come for him, or you, or me, as we wander together in this dark labyrinth of evil, stumbling at every step over the guilt we have scattered along our path. But that's not true! There could be good for you, and you alone, since you have been deeply wronged and have the power to forgive. Will you give up that unique privilege? Will you reject that invaluable gift?"

"Peace, Hester, peace!" the old man replied with dark severity. "I don't have the power to forgive. I lack the authority you speak of. My old beliefs, forgotten for so long, return to me now and make sense of everything we do and everything we endure. With your first misstep, you planted the seed of evil; but from that moment on, everything has been driven by dark inevitability. You who have wronged me are not truly sinful, except in some symbolic way; nor am I truly demonic, though I have taken on a demon's role. This is our destiny. Let the dark flower bloom however it will! Now go your way, and handle that man however you see fit."

He waved his hand and returned to his work of collecting

herbs.

Mandrake

Chapter 15: Hester and Pearl.

So Roger Chillingworth—a twisted old man with a face that lingered in people's memories far longer than they wanted—said goodbye to Hester Prynne and walked away hunched over along the ground. He picked up various herbs here and there, or dug up roots, placing them in the basket hanging from his arm. His gray beard nearly brushed the earth as he crawled forward. Hester watched him for a short time, observing with a somewhat strange curiosity to see if the delicate grass of early spring might wither beneath his feet, revealing the unsteady path of his steps as dried and brown marks across the bright green landscape. She wondered what kinds of herbs the old man was so carefully collecting. Wouldn't the earth, awakened to evil intentions by his watchful gaze, welcome him with toxic plants of previously unknown varieties that would spring up under his touch? Or would it be enough for him that every healthy plant should transform into something harmful and wicked at his contact? Did the sun, which shone so brilliantly everywhere else, actually reach him? Or was there, as it seemed more likely, a ring of threatening darkness that moved along with his twisted form, no matter which direction he faced? And where was he heading now? Wouldn't he suddenly disappear into the ground, leaving behind a barren and ruined patch where, eventually, deadly nightshade, dogwood, henbane, and whatever other poisonous plants the climate could grow would appear, all thriving with terrible abundance? Or would he unfold bat wings and fly away, appearing even more grotesque the higher he climbed toward heaven?

He collected herbs from various places

"Whether it's a sin or not," Hester Prynne said bitterly, as she continued to watch him, "I hate that man!"

She criticized herself for feeling this way, but couldn't overcome or reduce the emotion. As she tried to fight it, she remembered those long-ago days in a faraway place, when he would come out at evening from the privacy of his study and sit down by their home's firelight, bathed in the glow of her loving smile. He needed to warm himself in that smile, he told her, so that the coldness of all those solitary hours spent with his books could be lifted from his scholarly heart. Those moments had once seemed nothing but happy, but now, seen through the dark lens of her later life, they ranked among her most terrible memories. She wondered how such scenes could have ever happened! She wondered how she could have ever been convinced to marry him! She considered it the sin she most needed to repent—that she had ever tolerated and returned the halfhearted touch of his hand, and had allowed the smile from her lips and eyes to blend and dissolve into his. And it seemed like a more terrible wrong committed by Roger Chillingworth than anything that had been done to him since—that back when her heart didn't know any better, he had convinced her to imagine herself happy at his side.

"Yes, I hate him!" Hester said again, with even more bitterness than before. "He betrayed me! He has wronged me far worse than I ever wronged him!"

Let men fear pursuing a woman's hand in marriage unless they also capture the deepest passion of her heart! Otherwise, they may suffer the same wretched fate as Roger Chillingworth, discovering that when someone with a more powerful touch awakens all her emotions, they will be blamed even for the peaceful satisfaction and cold image of happiness they forced upon her instead of genuine warmth. But Hester should have moved past this unfairness long ago. What did this mean? Had seven long years of suffering under the punishment of the scarlet letter brought so much pain yet produced no remorse?

The feelings that swept through her during those few moments, as she watched the bent figure of old Roger Chillingworth disappear, cast a harsh light on Hester's mental state, exposing much that she might never have admitted to herself otherwise.

She called her child back to her after he had left.

"Pearl! Little Pearl!

Where are you?"

Pearl on the Sea-shore

Pearl, whose lively spirit never tired, had no trouble finding entertainment while her mother spoke with the old herb collector. At first, as already mentioned, she had playfully flirted with her own reflection in a pool of water, beckoning the phantom to come forward, and—when it refused to venture out—trying to find a way for herself into its world of untouchable earth and unreachable sky. Soon discovering, however, that either she or the reflection was not real, she looked elsewhere for better entertainment. She made small boats from birch bark, loaded them with snail shells, and launched more trading expeditions on the vast ocean than any merchant in New England; but most of them sank near the shore. She grabbed a live horseshoe crab by the tail, captured several starfish, and set out a jellyfish to dissolve in the warm sun. Then she picked up the white foam that marked the line of the incoming tide and threw it into the breeze, running after it with swift steps to catch the large snowflake-like pieces before they fell. Noticing a group of shore birds that fed and fluttered along the beach, the mischievous child filled her apron with pebbles and, crawling from rock to rock after these small seabirds, showed remarkable skill in throwing stones at them. One little gray bird with a white chest, Pearl was almost certain, had been struck by a pebble and flew away with a broken wing. But then the sprite-like child sighed and abandoned her game; because it saddened her to have hurt a small creature that was as free as the ocean breeze, or as free as Pearl herself.

Her last activity was to collect different types of seaweed and create a scarf or cloak and a headdress for herself, transforming her appearance into that of a small mermaid. She had inherited her mother's talent for creating clothing and costumes. As the finishing touch to her mermaid outfit, Pearl gathered some eel-grass and did her best to recreate on her own chest the decoration she knew so well from her mother's. A letter—the letter A—but bright green instead of scarlet! The child lowered her chin to her chest and studied this symbol with unusual fascination, as though the sole purpose for her existence in this world was to discover its secret meaning.

"I wonder if mother will ask me what it means?" thought Pearl.

Just then, she heard her mother's voice, and moving as gracefully as one of the small seabirds, she appeared before Hester Prynne, dancing, laughing, and pointing her finger at the decoration on her chest.

"My little Pearl," said Hester, after a moment's silence, "the green letter on your childish chest has no meaning. But do you know, my child, what this letter means that your mother is condemned to wear?"

"Yes, mother," said the child. "It is the great letter A. You have taught me in the primer."

Hester gazed intently at her little face, but despite noticing that peculiar expression she had observed so many times in her dark eyes, she couldn't determine whether Pearl truly understood what the symbol meant. She experienced an unhealthy urge to find out for certain.

"Do you know, child, why your mother wears this letter?"

"I really do!" Pearl replied, her face lighting up as she looked directly at her mother. "It's for the exact same reason that the minister always keeps his hand pressed over his heart!"

"And what reason is that?" Hester asked, half smiling at how absurdly mismatched the child's observation was; but after thinking about it for a moment, she turned pale. "What does the letter have to do with anyone's heart except mine?"

"No, mother, I have told you everything I know," said Pearl, speaking more seriously than she usually did. "Ask that old man you've been talking with! Maybe he can tell you. But really now, dear mother, what does this scarlet letter mean?—and why do you wear it on your chest?—and why does the minister keep his hand over his heart?"

She took her mother's hand in both of hers and looked into her eyes with a seriousness that was rarely seen in her wild and unpredictable nature. The thought came to Hester that the child might truly be trying to reach out to her with childlike trust, doing what she could, as thoughtfully as she knew how, to create a connection of understanding between them. This showed Pearl in an unusual light. Until now, the mother, while loving her child with the fierce devotion of someone whose heart belonged entirely to one person, had trained herself to expect little in return beyond the unpredictability of an April wind—one that spends its time in playful dancing, has sudden bursts of mysterious intensity, is moody even at its best, and more often brings a chill than warmth when you embrace it. In exchange for these troublesome behaviors, it will sometimes, following its own mysterious impulses, brush your cheek with uncertain gentleness, play softly with your hair, and then drift away to other aimless pursuits, leaving behind a wistful joy in your heart. And this, furthermore, was how a mother saw her child's temperament. Any other person watching might have noticed only unpleasant qualities and painted them in much darker tones. But now the thought came powerfully to Hester's mind that Pearl, with her extraordinary maturity and sharp intelligence, might already have reached an age where she could become a companion, someone who could be trusted with whatever portion of her mother's grief could be shared without disrespecting either parent or child. In the small turmoil of Pearl's personality, certain qualities might be emerging—and could have been visible from the very beginning—the solid foundations of unwavering bravery, an iron will, a fierce pride that could be shaped into dignity, and a harsh contempt for many things that, when closely examined, might prove to contain elements of dishonesty. She also had the capacity for love, though so far it had been sharp and unpleasant, like the complex tastes of fruit that hasn't yet ripened. With all these valuable qualities, Hester thought, the darkness that Pearl had inherited from her mother would have to be truly overwhelming to prevent a remarkable woman from emerging from this mysterious child.

Pearl's natural tendency to focus on the mystery of the scarlet letter seemed to be an essential part of who she was. From the very beginning of her conscious life, she had taken on this as her destined purpose. Hester had often imagined that Providence had a plan of justice and punishment in giving the child this distinct inclination; but never, until now, had she thought to ask whether, connected with that plan, there might also be a purpose of mercy and kindness. If little Pearl were regarded with faith and trust, as a spiritual messenger as well as an earthly child, might it not be her mission to ease away the sorrow that lay cold in her mother's heart, and had turned it into a tomb?—and to help her overcome the passion, once so intense, and even now neither dead nor sleeping, but only trapped within the same tomb-like heart?

These were some of the thoughts that now moved through Hester's mind, with such vivid intensity that they seemed to have been whispered directly into her ear. And there was little Pearl, during all this time, grasping her mother's hand with both of her own, and looking up at her face, as she asked these probing questions once, then again, and yet a third time.

"What does the letter mean, mother? And why do you wear it? And why does the minister keep his hand over his heart?"

"What should I say?" Hester thought to herself. "No! If this is the price of the child's sympathy, I cannot pay it."

Then she spoke aloud.

"Silly Pearl," she said, "what kind of questions are those? There are many things in this world that a child shouldn't ask about. What do I know about the minister's heart? And as for the scarlet letter, I wear it because of its gold thread."

Throughout all seven years that had passed, Hester Prynne had never been unfaithful to the symbol she wore on her chest. Perhaps it served as a charm from a harsh and unforgiving, yet protective spirit, who had now abandoned her; recognizing that despite keeping careful watch over her heart, some fresh evil had entered it, or some ancient wickedness had never been driven out. As for little Pearl, the seriousness quickly faded from her expression.

But the child wasn't ready to let the subject go. Two or three times on their way home, just as many times during dinner, and while Hester was tucking her into bed, and even once after she appeared to be sound asleep, Pearl looked up with mischief sparkling in her dark eyes.

"Mother," she said, "what does the scarlet letter mean?"

The next morning, the first sign that the child was awake came when she suddenly lifted her head from the pillow and asked that same question she had so mysteriously linked to her curiosity about the scarlet letter:

"Mother!—Mother!—Why does the minister keep his hand over his heart?"

"Keep quiet, you naughty child!" her mother replied, speaking more harshly than she had ever allowed herself to before. "Don't bother me, or I'll lock you in the dark closet!"

Chapter 16: A Forest Walk.

Hester Prynne stayed firm in her decision to reveal to Mr. Dimmesdale, regardless of any immediate pain or future consequences, the true nature of the man who had wormed his way into the minister's close friendship. For several days, though, she searched unsuccessfully for a chance to speak with him during one of his thoughtful walks that she knew he regularly took along the peninsula's shoreline or through the wooded hills of the surrounding countryside. There would have been no gossip, really, nor any danger to the sacred purity of the clergyman's reputation, if she had visited him in his private study, where many a repentant sinner had already confessed wrongdoings perhaps as serious as the one symbolized by the scarlet letter. But, partly because she feared the hidden or open meddling of old Roger Chillingworth, and partly because her guilty conscience imagined suspicion where none would have existed, and partly because both the minister and she would need all the space the vast world could offer to breathe freely while they spoke together—for all these reasons, Hester never considered meeting him in any more confined setting than under the open sky.

Finally, while helping in a sickroom where Reverend Mr. Dimmesdale had been called to offer a prayer, she discovered that he had left the previous day to visit the Apostle Eliot among his Indian converts. He would likely return by a specific time the following afternoon. Early the next day, therefore, Hester took little Pearl—who had to accompany her mother on all her journeys, no matter how awkward her presence might be—and departed.

The road, after the two travelers had crossed from the peninsula to the mainland, was nothing more than a footpath. It wandered forward into the mystery of the ancient forest. The forest enclosed it so tightly, and stood so black and thick on both sides, and revealed such incomplete glimpses of the sky above, that, to Hester's mind, it represented quite well the moral wilderness in which she had been wandering for so long. The day was cold and gloomy. Above was a gray stretch of cloud, stirred slightly, though, by a breeze; so that a flash of flickering sunshine could occasionally be seen in its lonely dance along the path. This passing cheerfulness was always at the far end of some long view through the forest. The playful sunlight—weakly playful, at best, in the prevailing sadness of the day and scene—pulled back as they approached, and left the places where it had danced more dreary, because they had hoped to find them bright.

"Mother," said little Pearl, "the sunshine doesn't love you. It runs away and hides because it's afraid of something on your chest. Look! There it is, playing far away. You stay here, and let me run and catch it. I'm just a child. It won't run from me because I don't wear anything on my chest yet!"

"And I hope it never will, my child," said Hester.

"And why not, mother?" asked Pearl, stopping suddenly just as she was about to start running. "Won't it come naturally when I become a grown woman?"

"Run away, child," her mother replied, "and catch the sunshine! It will be gone soon."

Pearl rushed forward with great speed, and Hester smiled as she watched her daughter actually catch the sunlight, standing there laughing surrounded by its glow, her whole being illuminated by its brilliance and sparkling with the energy that comes from quick movement. The light seemed to hover around the solitary child, as though it was delighted to have found such a companion, until her mother had come close enough to almost step into that enchanted circle as well.

"It will go now," said Pearl, shaking her head.

"Look!" Hester replied with a smile. "Now I can reach out my hand and grab some of it."

As she tried to do this, the sunlight disappeared; or, judging by the bright look that danced across Pearl's face, her mother might have imagined that the child had drawn it into herself, and would release it again, casting light on her path as they moved into darker shadows. No other quality impressed her mother so much with a sense of fresh and original energy in Pearl's character as this constant liveliness of spirit; she didn't suffer from the melancholy that nearly all children in these modern times inherit, along with other ailments, from their ancestors' hardships. Perhaps this too was an affliction, merely a reflection of the fierce determination with which Hester had battled her own sorrows before Pearl was born. It was definitely a questionable gift, giving the child's personality a harsh, cold shine. She lacked what some people need their entire lives—a deep sorrow that would touch her heart and make her more human and capable of understanding others' pain. But there was still plenty of time for little Pearl to experience such things.

"Come here, my child!" Hester called out, glancing around from where Pearl had stopped and was standing motionless in the bright sunlight. "We'll find a spot just inside the woods where we can sit down and take a rest."

"I'm not tired, mother," the little girl replied. "But you can sit down if you'll tell me a story while we rest."

"Tell me a story!" said Hester. "What should it be about?"

"Oh, a story about the Black Man," Pearl replied, grabbing onto her mother's dress and gazing up at her with an expression that was half serious, half playful. "About how he roams through this forest, carrying a book with him—a large, heavy book with iron clasps. And how this frightening Black Man offers his book and an iron pen to everyone he encounters here among the trees, and they must write their names using their own blood. Then he marks their chests! Have you ever met the Black Man, mother?"

"And who told you this story, Pearl?" asked her mother, recognizing a common superstition of the period.

"It was the old woman sitting by the fireplace at the house where you kept watch last night," said the child. "But she thought I was asleep while she was talking about it. She said that thousands and thousands of people had met him here, and had written in his book, and have his mark on them. And that bad-tempered lady, old Mistress Hibbins, was one of them. And, mother, the old woman said that this scarlet letter was the Black Man's mark on you, and that it glows like a red flame when you meet him at midnight, here in the dark woods. Is it true, mother? And do you go to meet him at night?"

"Did you ever wake up and find your mother gone?" asked Hester.

"I don't remember," said the child. "If you're afraid to leave me in our cottage, you could take me with you. I would really like to go! But, mother, tell me now! Is there really such a Black Man? And did you ever meet him? And is this his mark?"

"Will you leave me alone if I tell you just this once?" her mother asked.

"Yes, if you tell me everything," answered Pearl.

"I encountered the Black Man once in my lifetime!" her mother declared. "This scarlet letter is his sign!"

While talking, they walked deep enough into the woods to hide themselves from anyone who might pass by on the forest path. They sat down on a thick cushion of moss that had once been, sometime in the previous century, an enormous pine tree with its roots and trunk in the dark shadows and its top reaching high into the sky above. They had chosen a small hollow to rest in, with gentle slopes covered in fallen leaves rising on both sides and a stream running through the middle over a bed of dead and waterlogged leaves. The trees hanging overhead had dropped large branches over time, blocking the water's flow and forcing it to create whirlpools and dark pools in some places, while in the faster-moving sections, there was a clear path of pebbles and brown, glittering sand. Following the stream with their eyes, they could see light reflecting off the water a short distance into the forest, but soon lost sight of it among the confusing maze of tree trunks and undergrowth, with occasional massive rocks covered in gray lichens. All these enormous trees and granite boulders seemed determined to keep the path of this little stream a secret, perhaps worried that with its constant chatter, it might reveal secrets from deep within the ancient forest where it began, or show its discoveries on the calm surface of a quiet pool. As it moved along, the little stream kept up a constant murmur that was gentle, peaceful, and comforting, yet sad, like the voice of a young child growing up without joy, unable to find happiness among sorrowful companions and gloomy circumstances.

"Oh brook! Oh foolish and annoying little brook!" cried Pearl, after listening for a while to its babbling. "Why are you so sad? Cheer up, and don't spend all your time sighing and murmuring!"

But the brook, during its brief existence among the forest trees, had experienced something so profound that it couldn't stop talking about it, and appeared to have nothing else to discuss. Pearl was like the brook in that the flow of her life sprang from an equally mysterious source and had moved through scenes just as heavily shrouded in darkness. However, unlike the small stream, she danced and sparkled, and chattered cheerfully along her path.

"What is this sad little stream trying to tell us, mother?" she asked.

"If you had a sorrow of your own, the brook might tell you about it," her mother answered, "just as it is telling me about mine! But now, Pearl, I hear footsteps along the path, and the sound of someone pushing aside the branches. I want you to go play and leave me to speak with whoever is coming."

"Is it the Black Man?" asked Pearl.

"Will you go and play, child?" her mother repeated. "But don't wander far into the woods. And make sure you come when I call you the first time."

"Yes, mother," Pearl replied. "But if it's the Black Man, won't you let me stay for a moment and look at him with his big book under his arm?"

"Go on, silly child!" her mother said impatiently. "That's not the Black Man! You can see him now through the trees. It's the minister!"

"That's exactly right!" the child said. "And, mother, he's holding his hand over his heart! Is it because when the minister wrote his name in the book, the Black Man left his mark in that spot? But why doesn't he wear it on the outside of his chest, like you do, mother?"

"Go now, child, and you can tease me as much as you want another time," cried Hester Prynne. "But don't wander far. Stay where you can hear the babbling of the brook."

The child walked away singing, following the stream's path and trying to blend a more cheerful rhythm with its sad sound. But the little brook refused to be consoled, and continued sharing its mysterious secret about some very sorrowful event that had occurred—or making a prophetic cry about something that was still to come—somewhere within the boundaries of the gloomy forest. So Pearl, who already had enough darkness in her own small life, decided to end all connection with this complaining stream. She began picking violets and wood-anemones, along with some bright red columbines that she discovered growing in the cracks of a tall rock.

After her elf-child left, Hester Prynne took a step or two toward the path that wound through the forest, but she stayed beneath the thick shadows of the trees. She watched the minister walking along the trail, completely alone, leaning on a walking stick he had cut from the roadside. He appeared worn and weak, showing a helpless dejection in his manner that had never been so noticeably present during his walks around the settlement or in any other circumstances where he thought people might be watching him. Here, in the profound isolation of the forest—which by itself would have been a severe test of anyone's spirit—this despair was painfully obvious. His walk lacked energy, as though he couldn't see any point in taking another step forward and had no wish to continue, but would have been content, if he could feel content about anything, to throw himself down at the base of the closest tree and remain there motionless forever. The fallen leaves could cover him, and the earth could slowly pile up to create a small mound over his body, regardless of whether life remained in it or not. Death seemed too concrete a goal to either desire or try to escape.

To Hester's eye, Reverend Mr. Dimmesdale showed no signs of intense and lively suffering, except that, as little Pearl had noticed, he kept his hand pressed over his heart.

Chapter 17: The Pastor and His Parishioner.

Slowly as the minister walked, he had almost passed by before Hester Prynne could find her voice enough to get his attention. Finally, she managed to do so.

"Arthur Dimmesdale!" she said, weakly at first; then more loudly, but with a rough voice. "Arthur Dimmesdale!"

"Who's speaking?" the minister replied.

Quickly pulling himself together, he straightened up, like someone caught off guard in a state of mind he didn't want others to see. Looking nervously toward where the voice had come from, he could barely make out a figure beneath the trees, dressed in clothing so dark and blending so completely with the gray twilight that the overcast sky and thick leaves had brought to the middle of the day, that he couldn't tell if it was a woman or merely a shadow. Perhaps his journey through life was haunted in this way, by a ghost that had emerged from his own thoughts.

He took a step closer and spotted the scarlet letter.

"Hester! Hester Prynne!" he said. "Is that you? Are you alive?"

"Yes!" she replied. "In the kind of life I've lived these past seven years! And you, Arthur Dimmesdale, are you still alive?"

It was no surprise that they questioned whether each other truly existed in flesh and blood, and even doubted their own reality. They met so strangely in the shadowy forest that it felt like the first meeting in the afterlife between two souls who had been deeply connected in their previous existence, but now stood trembling with cold in mutual fear; unfamiliar with their current state and unaccustomed to the company of spirits without bodies. Each was a ghost, filled with wonder and terror at seeing the other ghost! They were equally amazed and frightened by themselves; because this critical moment reflected back their awareness and revealed to each heart its past and experiences, as life never does except during such intense, breathtaking moments. The soul saw its own reflection in the mirror of this fleeting instant. It was with fear, and shaking, and as if compelled by a slow, unwilling force, that Arthur Dimmesdale extended his hand, cold as death, and touched Hester Prynne's equally cold hand. That grip, cold though it was, removed the most depressing aspect of their meeting. They now felt themselves to be, at the very least, residents of the same world.

Without saying another word—neither taking the lead but moving with unspoken agreement—they drifted back into the shadowy woods where Hester had come from and settled on the pile of moss where she and Pearl had sat earlier. When they finally spoke, they began with the kind of casual comments and questions any two people who knew each other might exchange about the dark sky, the approaching storm, and then each other's well-being.

They moved forward this way, not boldly but gradually, toward the subjects that weighed most heavily on their minds. Having been kept apart so long by fate and circumstances, they needed these light, ordinary topics to go first and open the doors of conversation, so their true thoughts could eventually cross the threshold.

After some time, the minister focused his gaze directly on Hester Prynne's eyes.

"Hester," he said, "have you found peace?"

She smiled sadly, gazing down at her chest.

"Have you?" she asked.

"Nothing at all—only despair!" he replied. "What else could I expect, being who I am and living the kind of life I lead? If I were an atheist—a man without conscience—a person driven by crude and savage impulses—I might have found peace long ago. In fact, I never would have lost it in the first place! But given the state of my soul, whatever good qualities I originally possessed, all of God's most precious gifts have turned into sources of spiritual anguish. Hester, I am utterly wretched!"

"The people respect you," said Hester. "And surely you do good work among them! Doesn't this bring you any comfort?"

"More misery, Hester!—only the more misery!" the clergyman replied with a bitter smile. "When it comes to the good I might appear to accomplish, I have no faith in it. It has to be nothing but an illusion. What can a destroyed soul like mine achieve toward saving other souls?—or a corrupted soul toward making them pure? And regarding the people's reverence, I wish it would turn to contempt and hatred instead! Can you possibly think it's a comfort, Hester, that I must stand in my pulpit and face so many eyes looking up at me, as if heavenly light were shining from my face!—must watch my congregation starving for truth, and hanging on my every word as if one of the apostles were speaking!—and then look within myself and see the dark reality of what they worship? I have laughed, filled with bitterness and heartache, at the difference between how I appear and who I really am! And Satan laughs at it too!"

"You're being unfair to yourself," Hester said softly. "You have repented deeply and with great pain. Your sin belongs to the distant past. Your life now is truly as holy as it appears to others. Isn't there something real in repentance that has been confirmed and proven through good deeds? Why shouldn't that bring you peace?"

"No, Hester, no!" the clergyman replied. "There's nothing real in it! It's cold and lifeless, and it can't help me at all! I've done enough penance! But I've felt no true repentance! If I had, I would have cast off these robes of false righteousness long ago and revealed myself to the world as they'll see me on judgment day. You're fortunate, Hester, to wear the scarlet letter openly on your chest! Mine burns in secret! You have no idea what a relief it would be, after seven years of living this lie, to look into eyes that see me for who I truly am! If I had just one friend—or even my worst enemy—someone I could turn to daily when I'm sick of everyone else's praise, someone who would know me as the most wicked of all sinners, I think my soul might find a way to stay alive. Even that small amount of truth could save me! But now, everything is false!—everything is empty!—everything is death!"

Hester Prynne looked at his face but hesitated to speak. However, since he was expressing his long-suppressed emotions so intensely, his words gave her exactly the right moment to say what she had come to tell him. She overcame her fears and spoke.

"You have the kind of friend you just wished for," she said, "someone to share your tears over your sin—you have that in me, your partner in it!" She paused again, but forced herself to continue. "You've had such an enemy for a long time, and you live with him under the same roof!"

The minister jumped to his feet, gasping for air and clutching at his chest, as if he wanted to rip his heart right out of his body.

"Ha! What are you saying!" he cried. "An enemy! And under my own roof! What do you mean?"

Hester Prynne now fully understood the terrible harm she had caused this unfortunate man by allowing him to remain for so many years, or even for a single moment, at the mercy of someone whose intentions could only be evil. Simply being near his enemy, no matter what disguise the man might wear, was enough to disturb the spiritual balance of someone as sensitive as Arthur Dimmesdale. There had been a time when Hester was less aware of this reality; or perhaps, consumed by the bitterness of her own suffering, she had left the minister to endure what she imagined might be a more bearable fate. But recently, since the night of his vigil, all her feelings toward him had become both gentler and stronger. She now understood his heart more clearly. She had no doubt that Roger Chillingworth's constant presence—the hidden poison of his hatred contaminating the very air around him—and his official involvement as a doctor in the minister's physical and spiritual weaknesses—that these terrible opportunities had been used for a cruel purpose. Through these means, the suffering man's conscience had been kept in a state of constant agitation, which was designed not to heal through beneficial pain, but to destroy and corrupt his spiritual essence. The inevitable result on earth would almost certainly be madness, and in the afterlife, that eternal separation from all that is Good and True, of which insanity is perhaps the earthly representation.

This was the destruction she had caused the man who had once—no, why shouldn't we say it?—still loved her so deeply! Hester realized that sacrificing the minister's reputation, and even death itself, as she had already explained to Roger Chillingworth, would have been far better than the path she had decided to take. And now, instead of having to admit this terrible mistake, she would have willingly collapsed onto the forest floor and died right there at Arthur Dimmesdale's feet.

"Oh Arthur," she cried out, "please forgive me! In everything else, I have tried to be truthful! Truth was the one virtue I could have held onto, and did hold onto, through every hardship—except when your well-being, your life, your reputation were at stake! That's when I agreed to deceive you. But a lie is never right, even when death threatens from the other direction! Don't you understand what I'm trying to tell you? That old man—the doctor—the one they call Roger Chillingworth—he was my husband!"

Will you forgive me?

The minister stared at her for a moment with all the violent passion that—mixed with his nobler, purer, gentler qualities in various ways—was actually the part of him that the Devil claimed and through which he tried to win over the rest of his soul. Hester had never faced a darker or more fierce scowl than the one she saw now. For the brief moment it lasted, it was a sinister transformation. But his character had been so weakened by suffering that even his baser impulses could only manage a temporary fight. He collapsed to the ground and covered his face with his hands.

"I should have realized it," he whispered. "I did realize it! Wasn't the truth revealed to me through my heart's instinctive reaction the first time I saw him, and every time I've encountered him since? Why didn't I grasp what it meant? Oh Hester Prynne, you have no idea of the full horror of what has happened! And the humiliation!—the impropriety!—the terrible disgrace of having a diseased and guilty heart exposed to the very eyes that would take pleasure in seeing it! Woman, woman, you are responsible for this! I can never forgive you!"

"You have to forgive me!" cried Hester, throwing herself on the fallen leaves beside him. "Let God punish! You have to forgive!"

With sudden and desperate tenderness, she wrapped her arms around him and pressed his head against her chest, not caring that his cheek rested against the scarlet letter. He tried to pull away but couldn't manage to break free. Hester wouldn't let him go, afraid he might look at her with harsh judgment in his eyes. The entire world had looked down on her with disapproval—for seven long years it had scorned this solitary woman—and still she had endured it all, never once looking away with her steady, sorrowful gaze. Heaven, too, had shown its displeasure toward her, and yet she had survived. But the disapproval of this pale, frail, sinful, and grief-stricken man was something Hester could not endure and continue living!

"Will you forgive me?" she repeated, over and over again. "Won't you frown? Will you forgive?"

"I do forgive you, Hester," the minister finally replied, his voice heavy with deep sorrow but without any trace of anger. "I freely forgive you now. May God forgive us both! We are not the worst sinners in the world, Hester. There is someone worse than even a corrupted priest! That old man's revenge has been darker than my sin. He has deliberately violated the sacred nature of a human heart. You and I, Hester, never did such a thing!"

"Never, never!" she whispered. "What we did was sacred in its own way. We both felt it! We told each other so! Have you forgotten?"

"Quiet, Hester!" said Arthur Dimmesdale, getting up from the ground. "No; I haven't forgotten!"

They sat down once more, side by side with their hands clasped together, on the moss-covered trunk of the fallen tree. Life had never brought them a darker hour; this was the destination their path had been leading toward for so long, growing increasingly dim as it wound its way forward—and yet it held a magic that made them want to stay there, asking for one more moment, then another, and still another after that. The forest around them was dark and creaked with a wind that swept through it. The branches swayed heavily overhead, while one ancient tree groaned mournfully to another, as though sharing the sorrowful tale of the couple sitting below, or being forced to predict the misfortune yet to come.

And yet they stayed. How bleak the forest path looked that led back to the settlement, where Hester Prynne would have to shoulder once more the weight of her shame, and the minister would return to the empty pretense of his good reputation! So they remained a moment longer. No golden sunlight had ever been as valuable as the darkness of this shadowy forest. Here, witnessed only by his gaze, the scarlet letter didn't need to sear the chest of the disgraced woman! Here, seen only by her eyes, Arthur Dimmesdale, unfaithful to both God and humanity, could be, for just one moment, honest!

He was startled by a thought that suddenly came to him.

"Hester," he exclaimed, "this is a terrible new development! Roger Chillingworth knows that you plan to expose who he really is. Will he still keep our secret after this? What direction will his revenge take now?"

"There's something mysteriously secretive about him," Hester replied thoughtfully. "This trait has intensified through his hidden acts of revenge. I don't think he's likely to reveal the secret. He'll probably look for other ways to satisfy his dark obsession."

"And what about me!—how can I continue living, breathing the same air as this deadly enemy?" Arthur Dimmesdale cried out, recoiling into himself and pressing his hand anxiously against his heart—a movement that had become automatic for him.

"Think for me, Hester! You are strong. Decide for me!"

"You can't stay with this man any longer," Hester said slowly and firmly. "Your heart must no longer be under his evil influence!"

"It would be far worse than death!" the minister replied. "But how can I avoid it? What choice do I have left? Should I lie down again on these dried leaves, where I threw myself when you told me what he was? Must I collapse there and die immediately?"

"Oh no, look what's happened to you!" Hester said, tears flooding her eyes. "Are you going to die simply from weakness? There's no other reason!"

"God's judgment is upon me," replied the guilt-ridden priest. "It is too powerful for me to fight against!"

"Heaven would show mercy," Hester replied, "if only you had the strength to take advantage of it."

"Be strong for me!" he answered. "Tell me what to do."

"Is the world really so small?" Hester Prynne exclaimed, fixing her deep eyes on the minister's and instinctively wielding a magnetic power over a spirit so broken and defeated that it could barely keep itself upright. "Does the entire universe exist within the boundaries of that town over there, which just a short time ago was nothing but a leaf-covered desert, as desolate as this place around us? Where does that forest path lead? Back to the settlement, you say! Yes, but it also goes forward. It extends deeper and deeper into the wilderness, becoming less visible with each step, until just a few miles from here, the yellow leaves will show no trace of where white men have walked. There you would be free! Such a short journey would take you from a world where you have been utterly miserable to one where you could still find happiness! Isn't there enough shade in all this endless forest to hide your heart from Roger Chillingworth's watchful eyes?"

"Yes, Hester; but only under the fallen leaves!" the minister replied, with a sad smile.

"Then there's the wide ocean pathway!" Hester went on. "It carried you here. If you decide to, it will take you back again. In our homeland, whether in some distant country village or in enormous London—or certainly in Germany, in France, in beautiful Italy—you would be beyond his reach and awareness! And what do you have to do with all these rigid men and their judgments? They have already held your better nature captive for far too long!"

"That's impossible!" the minister replied, listening as though he were being asked to make a dream come true. "I don't have the strength to leave! As wretched and sinful as I am, I've had no other purpose than to continue my earthly life in the place where God has put me. Even though my own soul is lost, I would still do whatever I can for other people's souls! I don't dare abandon my position, even though I'm like an unfaithful guard whose certain punishment is death and disgrace when his miserable watch finally ends!"

"You've been crushed under seven years of misery," Hester replied, passionately determined to lift him up with her own strength. "But you can leave it all behind! It won't weigh down your steps as you walk through the forest path, and you won't have to carry it with you if you choose to sail across the ocean. Leave this destruction and ruin here where it happened. Don't deal with it anymore! Start completely fresh! Have you used up every possibility just because this one attempt failed? Absolutely not! The future is still full of opportunities for both struggle and success. There's happiness waiting to be experienced! There's good work to be accomplished! Trade this false life you're living for a genuine one. If your spirit calls you to such a purpose, become a teacher and messenger to the Native Americans. Or—since it suits your nature better—become a scholar and wise man among the most intelligent and famous people in the civilized world. Preach! Write! Take action! Do anything except lie down and give up! Abandon the name Arthur Dimmesdale and create a new identity for yourself, a noble one that you can carry without fear or shame. Why should you spend even one more day suffering these torments that have eaten away at your life—that have made you too weak to choose and to act—that will leave you unable even to feel remorse! Get up and go!"

"Oh Hester!" Arthur Dimmesdale cried out, his eyes showing a brief spark of hope that her passion had ignited before it quickly faded away. "You're talking about running a race to a man whose legs are shaking and can barely hold him up! I have to die here! I don't have the strength or the courage left in me to go out into the vast, unfamiliar, challenging world by myself!"

It was the final expression of despair from a shattered soul. He didn't have the strength to seize the better opportunities that appeared to be within his grasp.

He said the word again.

"Alone, Hester!"

"You will not go alone!" she answered in a deep whisper.

Then, everything was said!

Chapter 18: A Flood of Sunshine.

Arthur Dimmesdale looked into Hester's face with an expression that showed both hope and joy, but also fear mixed between them, along with a kind of horror at her boldness for saying what he had only vaguely suggested but hadn't dared to speak aloud.

But Hester Prynne possessed a naturally brave and active mind, and after being not just alienated but completely cast out from society for such an extended time, she had grown accustomed to a kind of free thinking that was completely foreign to the minister. She had wandered without rules or direction through a moral wasteland that was as vast, complex, and dark as the wild forest where they now sat having a conversation that would determine their destiny. Her mind and heart had made their home in these desolate places, where she roamed as freely as a wild Native American moves through his woodland territory. For years, she had observed human institutions from this outsider's perspective, along with everything that priests and lawmakers had created, judging them all with barely more respect than a Native American would show toward a minister's collar, a judge's robe, the public punishment platform, the execution scaffold, the family hearth, or the church building. The direction of her destiny and circumstances had worked to liberate her. The scarlet letter served as her pass into territories where other women wouldn't dare to venture. Shame, Despair, and Isolation had been her instructors—harsh and untamed teachers—and while they had made her resilient, they had also filled her education with serious flaws.

The minister, on the other hand, had never experienced anything that would push him beyond the boundaries of commonly accepted rules; though, on one occasion, he had terrifyingly violated one of the most sacred among them. But this had been a sin driven by passion, not by principle, or even by deliberate intent. Since that miserable time, he had monitored, with unhealthy intensity and attention to detail, not his actions—for those were easy to control—but every surge of feeling, and his every thought. Standing at the top of the social hierarchy, as clergymen of that era did, he was only more constrained by its rules, its principles, and even its biases. As a priest, the structure of his religious order inevitably confined him. As a man who had once committed sin, but who kept his conscience fully awake and painfully acute through the irritation of a wound that would not heal, he might have been considered more secure within the bounds of virtue than if he had never sinned at all.

Looking at Hester Prynne's situation, it appears that her entire seven years of exile and shame had served as nothing more than preparation for this exact moment. But what about Arthur Dimmesdale! If a man like him were to fall again, what excuse could possibly justify his wrongdoing? There would be none, unless it might help his case somewhat that he had been worn down by prolonged and intense suffering; that his judgment had become clouded and muddled by the very guilt that tormented him;

that when faced with the choice between running away as a confessed criminal or staying as a fraud, his conscience might struggle to decide which was right; that it was only natural to want to escape the threat of death and disgrace, along with the mysterious schemes of an adversary; that ultimately, this wretched wanderer on his bleak and lonely journey, weak, ill, and wretched, had caught sight of genuine human love and understanding, a fresh start and an honest one, in place of the terrible fate he was currently paying for. And let the harsh and sorrowful reality be stated clearly: once guilt has torn a hole in the human soul, it can never be completely healed in this earthly life. It can be monitored and protected so that the enemy cannot break through that same entrance again into the fortress, and he might even choose a different route in his future attacks rather than the one where he previously succeeded. But the damaged wall remains, and nearby lurks the quiet footsteps of the enemy who seeks to claim once more his unforgotten victory.

The struggle, if there was one, doesn't need to be described. It's enough to say that the clergyman decided to flee, and not by himself.

"If I could remember even one moment of peace or hope from these past seven years," he thought, "I would still endure this suffering for the sake of that promise of Heaven's mercy. But now—since I am beyond redemption—why shouldn't I take the comfort offered to a condemned prisoner before his execution? Or if this is truly the path to a better life, as Hester tries to convince me, I'm certainly not giving up any brighter future by following it! I can no longer live without her companionship; she has such power to support me and such tenderness to comfort me! O You to whom I dare not raise my eyes, will You still forgive me!"

"You will go!" said Hester, calmly, as he met her glance.

Once the decision was made, a strange sense of pleasure cast its wavering light over the turmoil in his chest. This was the thrilling effect—on a prisoner who had just broken free from the prison of his own heart—of breathing the wild, unrestricted air of an unrepentant, unchristian, lawless territory. His spirit seemed to leap upward and reached a closer view of the heavens than it had during all the suffering that had kept him crawling on the ground. Being deeply religious by nature, his mood inevitably carried a hint of spiritual devotion.

"Am I feeling joy again?" he cried out, amazed at himself. "I thought it had died within me! Oh Hester, you are my guardian angel! I feel as though I threw myself down—sick, stained with sin, and darkened by sorrow—onto these forest leaves, and have risen up completely renewed, with new strength to praise the One who has shown me mercy! This is already a better life! Why didn't we discover this sooner?"

"Let's not look back," Hester Prynne replied. "The past is over! Why should we dwell on it now? Look! With this symbol, I'm undoing everything and making it as if it never happened!"

As she spoke these words, she unfastened the clasp that held the scarlet letter in place, and removing it from her chest, she hurled it away among the dried, fallen leaves. The mysterious symbol landed on the near edge of the stream. If it had traveled just a hand's width further, it would have dropped into the water and given the small brook yet another sorrow to carry downstream, in addition to the mysterious story it continued to whisper about. But there the embroidered letter remained, sparkling like a lost gem that some unfortunate traveler might discover, and from that moment forward be tormented by eerie visions of guilt, feelings of despair, and unexplainable bad luck.

A Gleam of Sunshine

With the stigma removed, Hester let out a long, deep sigh as the weight of shame and pain lifted from her soul. What incredible relief! She hadn't realized how heavy the burden was until she experienced this newfound freedom! Acting on another impulse, she removed the stiff cap that held back her hair, and it cascaded down over her shoulders—dark and lustrous, carrying both shadow and light in its fullness, bringing a gentle softness to her face. A bright and loving smile played around her lips and shone from her eyes, seeming to flow from the very essence of her womanhood. A warm blush colored her cheek, which had been pale for so long. Her femininity, her youth, and all the richness of her beauty returned from what people call the unchangeable past, gathering together with her innocent hopes and a joy she had never known before, all within the magical boundaries of this moment. And as if the darkness of the earth and sky had simply been a reflection of these two human hearts, it disappeared along with their sadness. Suddenly, like a spontaneous smile from heaven, the sunshine broke through, flooding the dim forest with light, brightening every green leaf, turning the yellow fallen ones to gold, and streaming down the gray trunks of the majestic trees. The things that had created shadows before now held the light. The path of the small stream could be followed by its cheerful sparkle far into the mysterious heart of the woods, which had transformed into a mystery of happiness.

Such was nature's sympathy—that wild, untamed nature of the forest, never conquered by human law or enlightened by higher truth—with the joy of these two souls! Love, whether just beginning or awakened from a deathlike sleep, must always create sunshine, filling the heart so completely with light that it spills out into the world around us. Even if the forest had remained dark, it would have appeared bright to Hester's eyes, and bright to Arthur Dimmesdale's!

Hester looked at him with the excitement of a new happiness.

"You must know Pearl!" she said. "Our little Pearl! You have seen her—yes, I know it!—but you will see her now with different eyes. She is a strange child! I hardly understand her! But you will love her dearly, as I do, and will advise me how to deal with her."

"Do you think the child will be happy to know me?" asked the minister, somewhat uneasily. "I have long avoided children, because they often show distrust—a reluctance to be familiar with me. I have even been afraid of little Pearl!"

"Oh, that was so sad!" the mother replied. "But she will love you deeply, and you will love her too. She's not far away. I'll call her! Pearl! Pearl!"

"I can see the child," the minister said. "There she is, standing in a beam of sunlight, quite a distance away, on the far side of the stream. Do you think the child will love me?"

Hester smiled and once again called out to Pearl, who could be seen some distance away, exactly as the minister had described her—like a brilliantly dressed apparition standing in a shaft of sunlight that streamed down through an archway of tree branches. The light beam danced back and forth, causing her form to appear either faint or clear—sometimes like an actual child, other times like the ghost of a child—as the brightness faded and returned. She heard her mother calling and slowly made her way through the forest toward her.

Pearl hadn't found the time dragging while her mother sat talking with the minister. The vast dark forest—harsh as it appeared to those who brought their guilt and worldly troubles into its depths—became a companion to the solitary child, in whatever way it could. Dark though it was, it adopted its gentlest manner to welcome her. It offered her partridge-berries, grown during the previous autumn but only ripening in spring, now red as blood drops on the dried leaves. Pearl collected these and enjoyed their untamed taste. The small creatures of the wild barely bothered to step aside for her. A partridge, with ten chicks following behind, did rush forward in a threatening way, but quickly regretted her aggression and clucked to her babies not to fear. A pigeon, sitting alone on a low branch, let Pearl approach underneath and made a sound that seemed as much a greeting as a warning. A squirrel, from high up in his home tree, chattered either angrily or playfully—since a squirrel is such an irritable yet amusing little creature that distinguishing between his moods is difficult—so he chattered at the child and dropped a nut on her head. It was last year's nut, already nibbled by his sharp teeth. A fox, awakened from sleep by her soft footsteps on the leaves, looked curiously at Pearl, uncertain whether to sneak away or continue his nap in the same place. A wolf, it's claimed—though here the story surely becomes unlikely—approached and sniffed Pearl's dress, offering his wild head for her hand to pet. The truth appears to be, though, that the mother-forest and these untamed creatures it sustained all sensed a similar wildness in the human child.

And she was more gentle here than on the grass-bordered streets of the town, or in her mother's house. The flowers seemed to sense this; and one after another murmured as she walked by, "Decorate yourself with me, you beautiful child, decorate yourself with me!"—and, to delight them, Pearl picked the violets, and anemones, and columbines, and some branches of the brightest green, which the ancient trees lowered before her gaze. With these she adorned her hair, and her slender waist, and transformed into a woodland sprite, or a young tree spirit, or whatever else harmonized most closely with the ancient forest. In this manner had Pearl decorated herself, when she heard her mother's voice, and returned slowly.

Slowly; for she saw the clergyman.

Chapter 19: The Child at The Brook-Side.

"You will love her dearly," Hester Prynne repeated, as she and the minister sat watching little Pearl. "Don't you think she's beautiful?

And look at how naturally skilled she is at making those simple flowers decorate her! If she had gathered pearls, diamonds, and rubies in the woods, they couldn't have suited her any better. She's a magnificent child! But I know whose forehead she has!"

"Do you know, Hester," said Arthur Dimmesdale, with an uneasy smile, "that this dear child, always skipping around at your side, has caused me many moments of fear? I thought—Oh Hester, what a thought that is, and how terrible to fear it!—that my own features were partially reflected in her face, and so clearly that the world might recognize them! But she looks mostly like you!"

"No, no! Not mostly!" the mother replied with a gentle smile. "Just a little longer, and you won't need to be afraid to discover whose child she is. But how remarkably beautiful she looks with those wildflowers in her hair! It's as if one of the fairies we left behind in our beloved old England had dressed her up to greet us."

It was with a feeling that neither of them had ever experienced before that they sat and watched Pearl's slow approach. In her, the bond that connected them was clearly visible. She had been presented to the world for these past seven years as a living symbol, revealing the secret they so desperately tried to conceal—everything written in this sign—everything clearly apparent—if only there had been a prophet or magician skilled enough to interpret the character of flame! And Pearl represented the unity of their existence. Whatever past wrongdoing there might have been, how could they question that their earthly lives and future fates were linked when they saw before them both the physical union and the spiritual essence in whom they came together, and were destined to remain eternally united? Thoughts such as these—and perhaps other thoughts that they refused to admit or articulate—surrounded the child with a sense of wonder as she moved toward them.

"Don't let her see anything unusual—no intense feelings or

urgency—in how you approach her," Hester whispered. "Our Pearl is an unpredictable and whimsical little sprite at times. She's especially intolerant of emotions when she doesn't completely understand the reasons behind them. But the child has deep feelings! She loves me, and she will love you!"

"You can't imagine," said the minister, glancing sideways at Hester Prynne, "how much my heart fears this meeting, yet longs for it at the same time! But honestly, as I've already told you, children don't easily warm up to me. They won't climb onto my lap, or whisper in my ear, or respond to my smile; instead they keep their distance and look at me with strange expressions. Even tiny babies cry when I hold them in my arms. Yet Pearl, twice in her short life, has shown me kindness! The first time—you remember it well! The second was when you brought her with you to that stern old Governor's house."

"And you argued so courageously for both her and me!" the mother replied. "I remember it, and little Pearl will too. Don't worry! She might seem unusual and timid at first, but she'll quickly grow to love you!"

By this time Pearl had reached the edge of the brook and stood on the opposite side, gazing silently at Hester and the clergyman, who still sat together on the moss-covered fallen tree, waiting for her to come to them. Right where she had stopped, the brook happened to form a pool, so smooth and still that it reflected a perfect image of her small figure, with all the brilliant beauty of her appearance, decorated with flowers and woven leaves, but more refined and spiritual than the real thing. This reflection, so nearly identical to the living Pearl, seemed to give some of its own shadowy and mysterious quality to the child herself. It was strange, the way Pearl stood there, looking so intently at them through the dim light of the forest shadows; she herself, meanwhile, was bathed in a ray of sunshine that seemed drawn to her by some kind of natural attraction. In the brook below stood another child—

different yet the same—also touched by its ray of golden light. Hester felt herself, in some unclear and frustrating way, separated from Pearl; as if the child, during her solitary walk through the forest, had wandered out of the world in which she and her mother lived together, and was now trying unsuccessfully to return to it.

There was both truth and error in this impression; the child and mother had grown apart, but it was Hester's fault, not Pearl's. Since Pearl had wandered away from her side, another person had entered the circle of the mother's emotions, changing the nature of all her feelings so completely that Pearl, returning from her wandering, could not find her usual place and barely knew where she belonged.

"I have an odd feeling," said the troubled minister, "that this stream marks the border between two different worlds, and that you can never reunite with your Pearl again. Or perhaps she is some kind of supernatural being who, as the old stories from our youth told us, cannot cross flowing water? Please hurry her along; this waiting has already made me nervous."

"Come here, my dearest child!" Hester said encouragingly, stretching out both her arms. "You're moving so slowly! When have you ever been this hesitant before? Here is a friend of mine who must become your friend too. From now on, you'll have twice as much love as your mother alone could give you! Jump across the stream and come to us. You can leap like a young deer!"

The Child at the Brook-Side

Pearl ignored these sweet words completely and stayed on the far side of the stream. She looked intently at her mother with her bright, untamed eyes, then at the minister, then at both of them together, as though trying to understand and figure out what connection existed between them. For some mysterious reason, when Arthur Dimmesdale noticed the child watching him, his hand automatically moved to cover his heart—a gesture he had done so often it had become an unconscious habit. Finally, Pearl took on a strangely commanding presence, stretched out her hand with her little index finger pointing directly at her mother's chest. Below in the stream's reflection, the image of little Pearl appeared surrounded by flowers and sunlight, her small finger pointing as well.

"You strange child, why don't you come to me?" exclaimed Hester.

Pearl continued pointing with her finger, and a frown formed on her forehead, made even more striking by the childish, almost baby-like features that expressed it. As her mother kept gesturing for her to come and put on an unfamiliar display of cheerful smiles, the child stamped her foot with an even more commanding look and movement. In the stream, once again, appeared the magical beauty of the reflection, showing the same frown, pointing finger, and commanding gesture, emphasizing little Pearl's expression.

"Hurry up, Pearl, or I'm going to be angry with you!" called out Hester Prynne, who, despite being used to this kind of behavior from her mischievous child at other times, was understandably worried about her acting more appropriately right now. "Jump across the stream, you naughty child, and come over here! Otherwise I'll have to come get you myself!"

But Pearl wasn't frightened by her mother's threats or softened by her pleas. Instead, she suddenly exploded into a furious tantrum, waving her arms wildly and twisting her small body into the most dramatic positions. She accompanied this wild outburst with ear-piercing screams that echoed throughout the woods from every direction. Even though she was alone in her childish and irrational anger, it seemed as though an invisible crowd was supporting and encouraging her. In the stream below, Pearl's reflection appeared once again—a shadowy image decorated with flowers around her head and waist, but stamping her foot, gesturing frantically, and through it all, still pointing her tiny finger at Hester's chest!

“I understand what’s bothering the child,” Hester whispered to the minister, her face growing pale despite her determined effort to hide her distress and frustration. “Children cannot tolerate even the smallest change in the familiar appearance of things they see every day. Pearl notices that something is missing that she has always seen me wearing!”

“Please,” the minister replied, “if you have any way to calm the child, do it right now! Except for the bitter rage of an old witch, like Mistress Hibbins,” he added, trying to smile, “I know of nothing I would rather avoid than this fury in a child. In Pearl’s youthful beauty, just as in the wrinkled witch, it creates an unnatural effect. Calm her, if you love me!”

Hester looked back at Pearl, her cheeks flushing red as she glanced self-consciously at the minister, then let out a deep sigh; before she could even say a word, the flush drained from her face, leaving her deathly pale.

“Pearl,” she said sadly, “look down at your feet! There!—in front of you!—on this side of the stream!”

The child looked toward the spot her mother had pointed to, and there was the scarlet letter, lying so close to the edge of the stream that its gold embroidery shimmered in the water’s reflection.

“Bring it here!” said Hester.

“Come and take it yourself!” Pearl replied.

“What a child she is!” Hester remarked quietly to the minister. “Oh, I have so much to tell you about her! But honestly, she’s absolutely right about this horrible symbol. I have to endure its agony just a little while longer—only a few more days—until we’ve left this place behind and can look back at it like some land we only dreamed about. The forest can’t conceal it! The open ocean will take it from my hand and swallow it up forever!”

With these words, she walked to the edge of the stream, picked up the scarlet letter, and pinned it back onto her dress. Just moments before, when Hester had talked about throwing it into the deep ocean, she had felt hopeful, but now a sense of unavoidable fate settled over her as she took back this terrible symbol from destiny's hand. She had thrown it into endless space! She had breathed freely for one hour! And now here was the scarlet misery again, gleaming in its familiar place! This is always how it works, whether shown this way or not, that a wicked act takes on the nature of fate. Hester then gathered up the thick strands of her hair and tucked them under her cap. As if the sorrowful letter cast a destructive spell, her beauty, the warmth and fullness of her womanhood, vanished like disappearing sunlight; and a gray shadow seemed to settle over her.

When the grim transformation was complete, she reached out her hand to Pearl.

"Do you recognize your mother now, child?" she asked reproachfully, though her voice was quiet. "Will you cross the brook and acknowledge your mother, now that she bears her shame—now that she is filled with sorrow?"

"Yes; now I will!" the child answered, leaping across the stream and throwing her arms around Hester. "Now you are truly my mother! And I am your little Pearl!"

In a moment of unusual tenderness, she gently pulled her mother's head down and kissed her forehead and both cheeks. But then—driven by some inevitable force that always compelled this child to mix any comfort she might offer with a sharp pang of pain—Pearl lifted her lips and kissed the scarlet letter as well!

"That wasn't kind!" Hester said. "After you've shown me a little love, you mock me!"

"Why does the minister sit over there?" asked Pearl.

"He's waiting to welcome you," her mother replied. "Come, and ask for his blessing! He loves you, my little Pearl, and he loves your mother too. Won't you love him? Come! He's longing to greet you!"

"Does he love us?" said Pearl, looking up with sharp intelligence into her mother's face. "Will he go back with us, hand in hand, the three of us together, into the town?"

"Not right now, my dear child," Hester replied. "But someday he will walk alongside us, hand in hand. We'll have our own home with a warm fireplace, and you'll sit on his lap while he teaches you many things and loves you deeply. You'll love him too, won't you?"

"And will he always keep his hand over his heart?" asked Pearl.

"What a silly question!" her mother exclaimed. "Come and ask for his blessing!"

But whether driven by the jealousy that appears natural to every spoiled child when faced with a threatening rival, or due to some whim of her unpredictable personality, Pearl refused to show any kindness to the minister. Her mother had to use physical force to bring her close to him, as Pearl pulled back and displayed her unwillingness through strange facial expressions; she had mastered an unusual range of these since infancy, and could change her expressive face into a sequence of various looks, each one containing its own brand of mischief. The minister—uncomfortably embarrassed, but hoping that a kiss might serve as a charm to win the child's affection—leaned down and placed one on her forehead. At this, Pearl broke free from her mother and ran to the stream, where she bent down and washed her forehead until the unwanted kiss was completely removed and carried away by the flowing water. She then stayed at a distance, quietly observing Hester and the clergyman as they spoke together and made the plans that their new circumstances required and the goals they would soon accomplish.

And now this crucial meeting had come to an end. The small valley would be left empty among its dark, ancient trees, which, with their countless voices, would whisper for a long time about what had happened there, and no human would be any wiser. And the sorrowful stream would add this new story to the mystery that already weighed heavily on its small heart, and about which it continued its murmuring chatter, with no more cheerful tone than it had possessed for ages before.

I notice the heading you provided only contains "XX." which appears to be a section number or placeholder. There's no actual heading text to rewrite into contemporary English.

Could you please provide the complete heading you'd like me to rewrite?

The Minister in A Maze.

As the minister walked away, leaving Hester Prynne and little Pearl behind, he glanced back over his shoulder, half expecting to see only faint traces or outlines of the mother and child slowly disappearing into the gathering dusk of the forest. Such a dramatic change in his life couldn't immediately feel real to him. But Hester was still there, dressed in her gray gown, standing next to the fallen tree trunk that had been knocked down by some storm long ago, and which time had gradually covered with moss, creating a place where these two troubled souls, carrying life's heaviest burdens, could sit together and find a brief moment of peace and comfort. Pearl was there too, dancing lightly near the edge of the stream—now that the unwelcome stranger had left—and returning to her usual spot beside her mother. So the minister hadn't simply fallen asleep and dreamed it all!

To clear his mind of this confusion and conflicting feelings that troubled him with an unsettling restlessness, he remembered and carefully reviewed the plans that he and Hester had outlined for their escape. They had decided together that the Old World, with its crowded cities and populations, would provide them with better refuge and hiding places than the wilderness of New England or anywhere else in America, where their only options would be living in an Indian tent or staying in one of the few European settlements scattered sparsely along the coast. Beyond the minister's poor health, which wasn't strong enough to endure the harsh conditions of wilderness living, his natural talents, education, and complete personal development would only guarantee him a proper home within civilized and cultured society; the more advanced the society, the better suited he was to thrive in it. Supporting this decision, it happened that a ship was docked in the harbor—one of those dubious vessels common in those days that, while not exactly pirates, sailed the seas with a notable lack of accountability. This ship had just returned from the Spanish Main and would depart for Bristol within three days. Hester Prynne—whose work as a volunteer charitable helper had made her familiar with the captain and crew—could arrange passage for two adults and a child with all the discretion that their situation made absolutely necessary.

The minister had asked Hester, with considerable interest, exactly when the ship was expected to leave. It would likely depart on the fourth day from today. "How fortunate!" he had said to himself. Now, we hesitate to explain why Reverend Mr. Dimmesdale found this timing so very fortunate. However, to keep nothing from the reader, it was because he was scheduled to deliver the Election Sermon on the third day from today. Since such an occasion represented a distinguished milestone in any New England clergyman's life, he couldn't have found a better way or time to end his ministerial career. "At least people will say of me," this exemplary man thought, "that I left no public responsibility unfulfilled or poorly executed!" How tragic that such deep and sharp self-examination from this unfortunate minister should be so terribly misguided! We have revealed, and may yet reveal, worse things about him, but nothing, we believe, quite so pathetically weak. There exists no evidence so minor yet so undeniable of a hidden corruption that had long ago started consuming the true core of his character. No person can maintain one identity for himself and another for the public for any extended time without eventually becoming confused about which one is genuine.

The excitement of Mr. Dimmesdale's emotions as he returned from his meeting with Hester gave him unusual physical strength and pushed him toward town at a quick pace. The path through the woods seemed wilder and more rough with its crude natural barriers, and less walked upon by people, than he remembered it during his journey out. But he jumped across the muddy spots, pushed himself through the grabbing undergrowth, climbed the slopes, dove into the valleys, and conquered, in summary, all the challenges of the trail with a tireless energy that amazed him. He couldn't help but remember how weakly, and with how many frequent stops to catch his breath, he had struggled over the same ground just two days earlier. As he approached the town, he got a feeling of change from the sequence of familiar sights that appeared before him. It felt like not yesterday, not one or two, but many days, or even years ago, since he had left them. There, certainly, was each previous mark of the street as he remembered it, and all the distinctive features of the houses, with the proper number of peaked roofs, and a weather vane at every spot where his memory placed one. Nevertheless, this persistently intrusive feeling of change came over him. The same thing was true regarding the people he knew whom he encountered, and all the familiar forms of human life around the small town. They appeared neither older nor younger now; the beards of the elderly were no grayer, nor could the crawling baby from yesterday walk on his feet today; it was impossible to explain in what way they were different from the individuals on whom he had so recently given a farewell look; and yet the minister's deepest instinct seemed to tell him of their changeability. A similar feeling struck him most notably as he walked under the walls of his own church. The building had such a very strange, and yet so familiar, appearance that Mr. Dimmesdale's mind swayed between two thoughts; either that he had seen it only in a dream until now, or that he was simply dreaming about it at this moment.

This phenomenon, in all its different forms, showed no outward change, but revealed such a sudden and significant transformation in the observer of this familiar scene that the span of just one day had affected his awareness like the passing of years. The minister's own determination, along with Hester's resolve, and the destiny that developed between them, had brought about this change. The town remained the same as before; however, the same minister did not return from the forest. He could have told the friends who welcomed him, "I am not the person you believe me to be! I left him back there in the forest, hidden away in a secluded valley, beside a moss-covered fallen tree, and close to a sorrowful stream! Go find your minister, and see if his wasted body, his gaunt face, his pale, weary, grief-lined forehead, are not lying there like discarded clothing!" His friends would certainly have continued to argue with him, "You are indeed that very man!"—but they would have been mistaken, not him.

Before Mr. Dimmesdale reached home, his inner self showed him other signs of a complete transformation in his thoughts and emotions. In fact, nothing less than a total overthrow of leadership and moral principles in his inner world could explain the urges that now struck the troubled and shocked minister. With every step he took, he felt compelled to do something strange, wild, or wicked, with the feeling that it would be both uncontrollable and deliberate; against his will, yet arising from a deeper part of himself than the part that resisted the urge. For example, he encountered one of his own deacons. The good old man spoke to him with the fatherly love and elder's authority that his respected age, his honest and holy character, and his position in the Church gave him the right to use; and along with this, the deep, almost worshipful respect that the minister's professional and personal standing both required. There was never a more beautiful example of how the dignity of age and wisdom can exist alongside the submission and respect demanded of it, as from a lower social position and lesser gifts, toward a higher one. Now, during a conversation lasting two or three minutes between the Reverend Mr. Dimmesdale and this excellent and gray-bearded deacon, it was only through the most careful self-control that the former could stop himself from speaking certain blasphemous thoughts that came into his mind about the communion supper. He actually trembled and turned pale as ashes, afraid that his tongue might move on its own to speak these horrible ideas and claim his permission to do so without his actually giving it. And even with this fear in his heart, he could barely keep from laughing as he imagined how the holy old patriarchal deacon would have been shocked by his minister's irreverence!

Again, another incident of the same nature. Rushing down the street, Reverend Mr. Dimmesdale ran into the oldest female member of his congregation; a deeply religious and exemplary elderly woman; poor, widowed, alone, and with a heart as filled with memories of her deceased husband and children, and her long-dead friends, as a cemetery is filled with inscribed tombstones. Yet all of this, which would otherwise have been such crushing grief, was transformed into almost sacred joy for her devoted old spirit, through religious comfort and the truths of Scripture, which she had nourished herself with continuously for more than thirty years. And, since Mr. Dimmesdale had taken her under his spiritual care, the good grandmother's primary earthly comfort—which, unless it had also been a heavenly comfort, could not have been any comfort at all—was to encounter her pastor, whether by chance or by arrangement, and be renewed with a word of warm, sweet, heaven-sent Gospel truth, from his cherished lips, into her weakened, but joyfully attentive ear. But, on this occasion, up to the moment of placing his lips to the old woman's ear, Mr. Dimmesdale, as the great enemy of souls would have it, could remember no passage of Scripture, nor anything else, except a brief, sharp, and, as it seemed to him then, irrefutable argument against the immortality of the human soul. The planting of this idea in her mind would likely have caused this aged sister to fall down dead, immediately, as if from the effect of an extremely poisonous dose. What he actually did whisper, the minister could never afterward remember. There was, perhaps, a fortunate confusion in his speech, which failed to convey any clear idea to the good widow's understanding, or which Providence interpreted according to its own method. Certainly, as the minister looked back, he saw an expression of divine gratitude and rapture that seemed like the glow of the heavenly city on her face, so lined and pale as ash.

Again, a third instance. After leaving the old church member, he encountered the youngest sister of them all. She was a young woman recently converted—and converted by Reverend Mr. Dimmesdale's own sermon, on the Sunday following his vigil—to exchange the temporary pleasures of the world for heavenly hope, which would take on brighter form as life grew dark around her, and which would illuminate the complete darkness with final glory. She was beautiful and pure as a lily that had bloomed in Paradise. The minister knew well that he was himself treasured within the spotless sanctity of her heart, which draped its pure white curtains around his image, giving to religion the warmth of love, and to love a religious purity. Satan, that afternoon, had surely led the poor young woman away from her mother's side, and placed her in the path of this severely tempted, or—should we not rather say?—this lost and desperate man. As she approached, the arch-fiend whispered to him to compress into small space and drop into her tender heart a seed of evil that would be certain to bloom darkly soon, and bear black fruit in time. Such was his sense of power over this innocent soul, trusting him as she did, that the minister felt capable of destroying all the field of innocence with just one wicked look, and developing all its opposite with just a word. So—with a greater struggle than he had yet endured—he held his Geneva cloak before his face, and rushed onward, making no sign of recognition, and leaving the young sister to make sense of his rudeness as she might. She searched her conscience,—which was full of harmless little matters, like her pocket or her work-bag,—and blamed herself, poor thing! for a thousand imaginary faults; and went about her household duties with swollen eyelids the next morning.

Before the minister could celebrate his victory over this final temptation, he became aware of another urge, more ridiculous and nearly as terrible. It was—we are embarrassed to admit it—the impulse to stop right there in the street and teach some very profane words to a group of little Puritan children who were playing nearby and had only recently learned to speak. Resisting this bizarre impulse as beneath his position as a clergyman, he encountered a drunk sailor, one of the crew members from a ship that had sailed the Spanish Main. And here, since he had so courageously resisted all other forms of wickedness, poor Mr. Dimmesdale yearned, at the very least, to shake hands with this tar-stained scoundrel and entertain himself with some inappropriate jokes, the kind that immoral sailors have in abundance, along with a string of hearty, robust, solid, satisfying, and heaven-defying curses! It wasn't so much moral principle as it was partly his natural sense of propriety, and even more his rigid habit of ministerial dignity, that safely carried him through this latest crisis.

"What is it that torments and entices me like this?" the minister cried out to himself, finally stopping in the street and pressing his hand against his forehead. "Have I lost my mind? Or have I been completely surrendered to the devil? Did I make an agreement with him in the forest and seal it with my blood? And is he now calling me to honor it by urging me to commit every evil act that his most corrupt imagination can dream up?"

At the exact moment when Reverend Mr. Dimmesdale was having this internal conversation with himself and struck his forehead with his hand, old Mistress Hibbins, the notorious witch-lady, was reportedly walking by. She presented herself magnificently, wearing an elaborate headdress, an expensive velvet gown, and a ruff starched with the famous yellow starch whose secret her close friend Ann Turner had shared with her before that good lady was executed for the murder of Sir Thomas Overbury. Whether or not the witch had somehow read the minister's thoughts, she stopped completely, studied his face with keen perception, smiled cunningly, and—despite rarely engaging in conversation with clergymen—struck up a discussion.

"So, reverend Sir, you have visited the forest," the witch-lady remarked, nodding her tall headdress toward him. "Next time, I ask that you give me fair warning, and I would be honored to accompany you. Without presuming too much, my recommendation would go a long way toward ensuring any unfamiliar gentleman receives a warm welcome from that powerful figure you know of!"

"I declare, madam," the clergyman replied with a solemn bow, one that both the lady's social position required and his own proper upbringing demanded, "I declare, on my conscience and reputation, that I am completely confused about what you mean! I did not go into the forest to seek out a ruler; nor do I plan to visit there in the future with any intention of winning favor from such a person. My only purpose was to meet my devout friend, the Apostle Eliot, and celebrate with him the many precious souls he has converted from paganism!"

"Ha, ha, ha!" cackled the old witch-woman, still nodding her tall headdress at the minister. "Well, well, we must talk this way during the day! You handle it like an expert! But at midnight, in the forest, we'll have a very different conversation!"

She continued on with her dignified, elderly grace, but frequently looked back over her shoulder and smiled at him, like someone ready to acknowledge a private, intimate bond between them.

"Have I sold my soul," the minister wondered, "to the devil who, if people are telling the truth, this yellow-starched and velvet-wearing old witch has chosen as her prince and master!"

The miserable minister! He had struck a deal very much like it! Lured by a vision of happiness, he had surrendered himself, through conscious decision, as he never had before, to what he understood was mortal sin. And the spreading poison of that sin had spread so quickly through his entire moral being. It had numbed all virtuous impulses and brought to intense life the complete family of evil ones. Contempt, resentment, unprompted hatred, needless craving for harm, mockery of anything good and sacred, all stirred to life, tempting him even as they terrified him. And his meeting with old Mistress Hibbins, if it was a genuine event, only revealed his connection and kinship with sinful people and the realm of corrupted souls.

He had, by this time, reached his home, on the edge of the cemetery, and, hurrying up the stairs, took shelter in his study. The minister was relieved to have reached this sanctuary, without first exposing himself to the world through any of those strange and sinful impulses that had constantly urged him while walking through the streets. He entered the familiar room, and looked around at its books, its windows, its fireplace, and the tapestried comfort of the walls, with the same sense of strangeness that had followed him throughout his walk from the forest clearing into the town, and back again. Here he had studied and written; here, endured fasting and sleepless nights, and emerged half dead; here, struggled to pray; here, suffered countless torments! There was the Bible, in its rich old Hebrew, with Moses and the Prophets speaking to him, and God's voice through all! There, on the table, with the ink-stained pen beside it, was an unfinished sermon, with a sentence broken in the middle, where his thoughts had stopped flowing onto the page, two days earlier. He knew that it was himself, the thin and pale-faced minister, who had done and endured these things, and written this far into the Election Sermon! But he seemed to stand apart, and observe this former self with scornful, pitying, but half-jealous curiosity. That self was gone. Another man had returned from the forest; a wiser one; with knowledge of hidden mysteries which the innocence of the former could never have grasped. A bitter kind of knowledge that!

While he was lost in these thoughts, someone knocked at the study door, and the minister called out, "Come in!"—not entirely free from the notion that he might see an evil spirit. And indeed he did! It was old Roger Chillingworth who walked in. The minister stood there, pale and unable to speak, with one hand resting on the Hebrew Scriptures and the other pressed against his chest.

"Welcome home, reverend Sir," the physician said. "How did you find that godly man, the Apostle Eliot? But I think, dear Sir, you look pale, as if the journey through the wilderness has been too difficult for you. Won't you need my help to restore your spirit and strength so you can preach your Election Sermon?"

"No, I don't think so," replied Reverend Mr. Dimmesdale. "My journey, and seeing the holy Apostle over there, and the fresh air I've been breathing, have done me good after being confined in my study for so long. I don't think I need any more of your medicines, my kind physician, even though they are good and given by a friendly hand."

All this time, Roger Chillingworth was studying the minister with the serious and focused attention of a doctor examining his patient. However, despite this outward appearance, the minister was almost certain that the old man knew about, or at least strongly suspected, his secret meeting with Hester Prynne. The physician understood that in the minister's eyes, he was no longer a trusted friend, but rather his most bitter enemy. With so much now understood between them, it would seem natural for some of this tension to be spoken aloud. It's strange, though, how much time often goes by before words actually give voice to reality; and how safely two people who want to avoid a particular topic can come right to the edge of discussing it and then pull back without ever addressing it directly. Therefore, the minister felt no fear that Roger Chillingworth would speak openly about the true relationship that existed between them. Yet the physician, in his sinister way, came terrifyingly close to revealing the secret.

"Wouldn't it be better," he said, "if you used my humble skills tonight? Truly, dear Sir, we must make an effort to ensure you're strong and energetic for this Election Day sermon. The people are expecting great things from you, fearing that another year might pass and they'll find their pastor has died."

"Yes, to another world," the minister replied with devout acceptance. "Heaven grant that it will be a better one; for truly, I hardly expect to remain with my congregation through the changing seasons of another year! But regarding your medicine, kind Sir, in my current physical condition, I do not need it."

"I'm delighted to hear that," the physician replied. "Perhaps my treatments, which I've been giving for so long without success, are finally starting to work properly. I would be a fortunate man indeed, and truly worthy of New England's appreciation, if I could accomplish this healing!"

"I thank you from the bottom of my heart, my most vigilant friend," said Reverend Mr. Dimmesdale, with a serious smile. "I thank you, and I can only repay your good deeds with my prayers."

"A good man's prayers are worth their weight in gold!" old Roger Chillingworth replied as he departed. "Yes, they're like the official currency of the New Jerusalem, bearing the King's own seal of approval!"

Left alone, the minister called for a household servant and asked for food, which was brought to him, and he devoured it hungrily. Then, throwing the already completed pages of the Election Sermon into the fire, he immediately started writing another one, composing it with such a passionate rush of thoughts and feelings that he believed himself to be divinely inspired; he could only marvel that Heaven would choose to deliver the magnificent and sacred music of its divine messages through such a corrupted vessel as himself. Nevertheless, leaving that puzzle to resolve itself or remain forever unsolved, he pressed forward with his work, driven by urgent determination and spiritual rapture. In this way the night passed swiftly, as though it were a flying horse that he was riding; morning arrived and appeared shyly through the curtains; and finally sunrise cast a golden ray into the study, falling directly across the minister's dazzled eyes. There he sat, still holding the pen in his hand, with an enormous, boundless expanse of written pages spread out behind him!

Chapter 21: The New England Holiday.

Early in the morning on the day when the new Governor was to be sworn into office by the people, Hester Prynne and little Pearl entered the marketplace. The area was already crowded with craftsmen and other common residents of the town in large numbers; among them were also many rugged figures whose deerskin clothing identified them as coming from the forest settlements that surrounded the small capital of the colony.

On this public holiday, just like every other day for the past seven years, Hester wore a dress made of rough gray fabric. The color and the strange way it was cut made her seem to disappear, as if she were fading into the background. But then the scarlet letter would pull her back from this shadowy invisibility, revealing her in the harsh light of its moral judgment. Her face, which the townspeople had grown so used to seeing, showed the same stone-like calm they always expected. It was like wearing a mask, or more accurately, like the frozen stillness you see on a dead person's face. This grim comparison fit because Hester was essentially dead to the world around her—cut off from any hope of compassion, she had withdrawn from the community she still appeared to be part of.

Perhaps on this particular day, there was an expression that had never appeared before, though it wasn't clear enough to notice now unless someone with extraordinary perception had first understood her heart and then looked for matching signs in her face and bearing. Such a spiritually gifted observer might have realized that after enduring the stare of the crowd for seven terrible years as something necessary, as punishment, and as something her strict sense of duty demanded she bear, she now faced it one final time freely and by choice, wanting to transform what had been agony for so long into a kind of victory. "Take your last look at the scarlet letter and the woman who wears it!" the people's victim and lifelong prisoner, as they imagined her to be, might have said to them. "Soon she will be beyond your reach! In just a few more hours, the deep, mysterious ocean will extinguish and hide forever the symbol you have made burn on her chest!" It wouldn't be too unlikely for human nature if we imagined that Hester felt some regret at the moment she was about to gain freedom from the pain that had become so deeply woven into her very existence. Might there not be an overwhelming urge to drink one last, long, breathless gulp from the cup of bitterness and suffering that had constantly flavored nearly all her adult years? The wine of life that would be offered to her from now on would need to be truly rich, delicious, and thrilling in its ornate golden cup, or else it would leave behind an inevitable and weary emptiness after the bitter dregs she had been fed, as if they were a medicine of the strongest kind.

Pearl was dressed with light-hearted cheerfulness. It would have been impossible to imagine that this bright and sunny figure came from someone clothed in somber gray, or that the same imagination that created such gorgeous and delicate clothing for the child had also accomplished perhaps an even more challenging task by giving such distinctive character to Hester's simple dress. Pearl's outfit seemed so perfectly suited to her that it appeared to flow naturally from her being, an inevitable expression of her inner nature, no more separable from her than the multicolored brilliance of a butterfly's wing or the vibrant beauty of a flower's petal. Just as with these natural wonders, the child's clothing was completely in harmony with her essence. On this significant day, there was also a particular restlessness and excitement in her demeanor, much like the sparkle of a diamond that glitters and flashes with the changing rhythms of the heart beneath it. Children always share in the emotional disturbances of those close to them, and they're especially sensitive to any trouble or approaching change in their home life. Therefore Pearl, who was like a precious jewel resting on her mother's troubled heart, revealed through her very liveliness the feelings that no one could see in the stone-like calmness of Hester's face.

This bubbling energy made her dart around with quick, bird-like movements instead of walking calmly beside her mother. She constantly burst into wild, wordless cries that sometimes became sharp and piercing sounds. When they arrived at the market-place, she grew even more restless as she noticed the activity and commotion that brought life to the area; normally it resembled the wide, empty grass space in front of a village meeting-house more than the busy heart of a town's commerce.

"Why, what is this, mother?" she cried. "Why have all the people stopped working today? Is it a holiday for everyone? Look, there's the blacksmith! He's washed his dirty face and put on his

Sunday clothes, and he looks like he'd love to celebrate if someone would just show him how! And there's Master Brackett, the old jailer, nodding and smiling at me. Why is he doing that, mother?"

"He remembers you as a little baby, my child," Hester replied.

"He shouldn't nod and smile at me like that—that dark, stern, ugly-eyed old man!" Pearl said. "He can nod at you if he wants to, since you're dressed in gray and wearing the scarlet letter. But look, mother, at all these faces of strange people, with Indians and sailors among them! Why have they all come here to the marketplace?"

"They're waiting to watch the parade go by," Hester explained. "The Governor and the magistrates will be passing through, along with the ministers and all the important and respected people, with music playing and soldiers marching ahead of them."

"And will the minister be there?" asked Pearl. "And will he reach out both his hands to me, like he did when you brought me to him from the stream?"

"He will be there, child," her mother replied. "But he won't acknowledge you today, and you must not acknowledge him either."

"What a strange, sad man he is!" said the child, as if speaking partly to herself. "In the dark nighttime he calls us to him, and holds your hand and mine, just like when we stood with him on that scaffold over there. And in the deep forest, where only the old trees can hear, and the strip of sky can see it, he talks with you, sitting on a pile of moss! And he kisses my forehead, too, so much that the little brook could hardly wash it off! But here, in the sunny daylight, and among all the people, he doesn't know us; and we must not know him! He is a strange, sad man, with his hand always over his heart!"

"Be quiet, Pearl! You don't understand these things," said her mother. "Don't think about the minister right now, but look around you, and see how cheerful everyone's face is today. The children have come from their schools, and the adults from their workshops and their fields, specifically to be happy. For today, a new man is beginning to rule over them; and so—as has been the custom of humanity ever since a nation was first formed—they celebrate and rejoice; as if a good and golden year were finally going to pass over the poor old world!"

It was just as Hester had observed regarding the unusual cheerfulness that lit up people's faces. During this festive time of year—which it already was, and would remain for most of the next two centuries—the Puritans packed together whatever happiness and public celebration they considered acceptable for human weakness; in doing so, they temporarily lifted their usual somber mood enough that, for the duration of one holiday, they seemed hardly more serious than most other communities during times of widespread hardship.

But we might be overstating the dark or somber tone that certainly marked the mood and customs of that era. The people now gathered in Boston's marketplace hadn't been born into a legacy of Puritan gloominess. They were native Englishmen whose ancestors had lived during the bright prosperity of the Elizabethan age—a period when English life, considered as a whole, seemed to have been as grand, magnificent, and joyful as the world has ever seen. If they had followed their inherited preferences, the New England colonists would have marked all significant public events with bonfires, feasts, elaborate displays, and parades. It wouldn't have been impossible, when observing grand ceremonies, to blend cheerful entertainment with seriousness, creating what could be described as colorful and striking decoration for the great ceremonial garment that a nation wears during such celebrations. There was some hint of this kind of attempt in how they celebrated the day when the colony's political year began. The faint echo of remembered grandeur—a pale and greatly watered-down version of what they had witnessed in magnificent old London, not necessarily at a royal coronation, but perhaps at a Lord Mayor's parade—could be seen in the traditions our ancestors established for the yearly installation of government officials. The fathers and founders of the commonwealth—the politicians, clergy, and military leaders—considered it their responsibility to display the external dignity and grandeur that, according to traditional custom, was viewed as the appropriate dress for those holding public or social prominence. They all emerged to march in procession before the people's eyes, thereby lending necessary dignity to the basic structure of such a newly formed government.

Then, too, the people were allowed, if not actively encouraged, to ease up on the strict and intense dedication to their various forms of harsh labor, which, at all other times, seemed to be cut from the same cloth as their religion. Here, it is true, there were none of the entertainments that popular festivities would have so easily provided in Elizabeth's England, or during James's reign—no crude theatrical performances; no minstrel with his harp and traditional songs, nor entertainer with a monkey dancing to his music; no performer with his tricks of mock magic; no comic fool to rouse the crowd with jokes, perhaps centuries old, but still powerful in their appeal to the most basic sources of humorous connection. All such practitioners of the various forms of entertainment would have been harshly suppressed, not only by the strict enforcement of law, but by the general attitude that gives law its strength. Nevertheless, the great, sincere face of the people smiled, perhaps grimly, but broadly as well. Nor were activities lacking, such as the colonists had witnessed and participated in long ago at the country fairs and village greens of England; activities that were considered important to maintain on this new land, for the sake of the bravery and strength of character that were vital to them. Wrestling matches, in the different styles of Cornwall and Devonshire, could be seen here and there around the marketplace; in one corner, there was a friendly contest with quarterstaffs; and—what drew the most attention of all—on the platform of the pillory, already so prominent in our story, two masters of combat were beginning a demonstration with shield and broadsword. But, much to the crowd's disappointment, this last event was interrupted by the intervention of the town officer, who had no intention of allowing the dignity of the law to be undermined by such misuse of one of its sacred places.

It might not be going too far to say that, overall, these people—who were still in the early stages of their somber behavior and were the children of fathers who had known how to celebrate and be cheerful in their time—would actually compare well with their descendants in terms of celebrating holidays, even with people as far removed as ourselves. The generation that came immediately after them, the children of those early settlers, embraced the darkest form of Puritanism and cast such a shadow over the national character that all the years since then have not been enough to lift it. We still need to relearn the lost art of joy and celebration.

The scene of human life in the marketplace, while generally colored in the somber gray, brown, or black of the English settlers, was brightened by some variety of color. A group of Indians—dressed in their wild finery of intricately embroidered deerskin robes, wampum belts, red and yellow ochre paint, and feathers, and carrying bows and arrows and stone-tipped spears—stood by themselves, their faces showing an unyielding seriousness that surpassed even what the Puritan expression could achieve. Yet, as wild as these painted natives were, they weren't the most untamed element of the scene. This honor could more accurately be given to some sailors—part of the crew from a ship that had sailed from the Spanish Main—who had come to shore to witness the festivities of Election Day. They were rough-looking outlaws with sun-darkened faces and enormous beards; their loose, short pants were held at the waist by belts, often fastened with crude gold buckles, and always supporting a long knife, and sometimes a sword. From under their wide-brimmed palm-leaf hats shone eyes that, even when showing good humor and joy, held a kind of wild brutality. They violated, without fear or hesitation, the behavioral standards that bound everyone else; they smoked tobacco right under the church officer's nose, though each puff would have cost a local resident a shilling; and they drank freely from flasks of wine or strong liquor from their pockets, which they generously offered to the staring crowd surrounding them. It notably revealed the flawed morality of that era, strict though we consider it, that sailors were permitted such freedom, not only for their wild behavior on land, but for far more dangerous acts on the sea. The sailor of that time would nearly be charged as a pirate by today's standards. There could be little question, for example, that this very ship's crew, though they weren't particularly bad examples of seafaring men, had committed what we would call raids on Spanish merchant ships, acts that would have endangered all their lives in a modern courtroom.

But the ocean in those earlier times rose, surged, and churned largely according to its own nature, or influenced only by stormy winds, with virtually no efforts at control by human laws. A pirate on the waters could abandon his profession and immediately become, if he wished, a man of honor and devotion on shore; furthermore, even while actively pursuing his reckless lifestyle, he wasn't considered someone it would be shameful to do business with or spend time around. Therefore, the Puritan leaders, dressed in their black robes, stiff collars, and tall pointed hats, looked with reasonable favor upon the noise and crude behavior of these cheerful sailors; and it caused neither shock nor criticism when such a respected citizen as old Roger Chillingworth, the doctor, was observed entering the marketplace while engaged in intimate and friendly conversation with the captain of the suspicious ship.

The latter was by far the most impressive and dashing figure in terms of clothing that could be seen anywhere among the crowd. He wore an abundance of ribbons on his outfit, and gold trim on his hat, which was also surrounded by a gold chain and topped with a feather. There was a sword at his side, and a sword wound on his forehead, which, by the way he arranged his hair, he seemed eager to show off rather than conceal. A person from land could hardly have worn this outfit and displayed this face, and worn and shown them both with such a bold manner, without facing harsh questioning before a judge, and probably receiving a fine or jail time, or perhaps being put on display in the stocks. As for the ship captain, however, everything was seen as fitting his role, just as natural as a fish having shimmering scales.

After leaving the doctor, the captain of the Bristol ship wandered aimlessly through the marketplace until he happened to come near the place where Hester Prynne was standing. He seemed to recognize her and didn't hesitate to speak with her. As always happened wherever Hester stood, a small empty space—like a magical circle—had formed around her. Even though people were pushing against each other just a short distance away, no one dared or wanted to step into this circle. This was a powerful symbol of the moral isolation that the scarlet letter created around the person forced to wear it, caused partly by her own reserved nature and partly by the instinctive, though no longer cruel, withdrawal of other people. Now, if never before, this served a useful purpose by allowing Hester and the sailor to talk together without the risk of being overheard. Hester Prynne's reputation with the public had changed so much that even the most respected woman in town, known for her strict moral standards, could not have had such a conversation with less chance of causing gossip than Hester herself.

Chillingworth—Smile with a sinister meaning

"So, madam," said the sailor, "I must tell the steward to

prepare one more sleeping quarters than you arranged for! No worry about scurvy or ship fever on this voyage! What with the ship's doctor and this other physician, our only danger will be from medicine or pills; especially since there's a lot of pharmacy supplies on board, which I obtained through trade with a Spanish ship."

"What do you mean?" asked Hester, more startled than she allowed herself to show. "Do you have another passenger?"

"Don't you know," shouted the ship captain, "that this doctor here—Chillingworth, he calls himself—plans to share my cabin accommodations with you? Yes, yes, you must have known this; he told me he's part of your group, and a close friend to the gentleman you mentioned—the one who's in danger from these bitter old Puritan leaders!"

"They know each other well, indeed," Hester replied, maintaining a calm appearance despite being utterly alarmed. "They have lived together for a long time."

Nothing more was said between the sailor and Hester Prynne. But at that moment, she saw old Roger Chillingworth himself, standing in the farthest corner of the marketplace, smiling at her; a smile that—across the wide and busy square, and through all the conversation and laughter, and the different thoughts, feelings, and concerns of the crowd—carried a secret and frightening message.

Chapter 22: The Procession.

Before Hester Prynne could gather her thoughts and figure out what she could actually do about this shocking new turn of events, she heard military music coming from a nearby street. The sound announced that the procession of magistrates and citizens was approaching, heading toward the meeting-house where Reverend Mr. Dimmesdale would deliver an Election Sermon, following a tradition that had been established early on and continued ever since.

Soon the front of the procession came into view, moving with a slow and dignified pace as it turned the corner and made its way across the marketplace. The music came first. It included various instruments that perhaps didn't blend perfectly together and weren't played with exceptional skill, yet they achieved the main purpose that drum and trumpet music serves for crowds—giving a more elevated and heroic quality to the scene of life unfolding before people's eyes. Little Pearl initially clapped her hands, but then momentarily lost the restless energy that had kept her in constant excitement all morning; she watched quietly and seemed to be lifted up, like a floating seabird, on the long rises and falls of the music. However, she returned to her previous mood when she saw the glint of sunlight on the weapons and shining armor of the military company that followed the musicians and served as the ceremonial guard for the procession. This group of soldiers—which still exists as an organization and marches forward from earlier times with an ancient and respected reputation—wasn't made up of hired fighters. Its members were gentlemen who felt the call of military spirit and wanted to create a kind of military academy where, like an order of Knights Templars, they could study the theory and, as much as peacetime training would allow, the practice of warfare. The high respect given to military character at that time could be seen in the proud bearing of each member of the company. Some of them had actually earned their right to take on the title and ceremony of soldiers through their service in the Netherlands and other European battlefields. The whole formation, dressed in polished steel armor with feathers waving above their bright helmets, created a spectacular sight that no modern military display could hope to match.

The distinguished civilians who followed directly behind the military procession deserved far more attention from any thoughtful observer. Even in their outward appearance, they displayed a natural authority that made the soldiers' proud marching seem crude, even ridiculous. This was a time when what we now call talent received much less recognition than it does today, but the substantial qualities that create stable and dignified character were valued far more highly. The people naturally possessed an inherited sense of reverence—a quality that, among their descendants today, exists in much smaller measure and with greatly reduced strength when choosing and evaluating public leaders. This transformation may be beneficial or harmful, and likely represents some of both. In those early days, the English colonists on these harsh coastlines had left behind their king, nobility, and all forms of imposing social hierarchy, yet they still felt a strong capacity and need for reverence. They directed this respect toward the white hair and dignified faces of the elderly, toward proven integrity, toward sound judgment and hard-earned experience, and toward those serious and substantial qualities that suggest permanence and fall under the broad category of respectability. These early political leaders—Bradstreet, Endicott, Dudley, Bellingham, and their colleagues—who rose to positions of authority through the people's early selections, appear to have been not particularly brilliant, but notable for their weighty seriousness rather than mental agility. They possessed courage and independence, and during times of trouble or danger, they defended the colony's interests like a wall of stone cliffs standing firm against a violent storm. The character traits described here were clearly visible in the square-jawed faces and imposing physical presence of these new colonial officials. In terms of displaying natural leadership, the mother country would not have felt embarrassed to see these leading figures of a functioning democracy welcomed into the House of Peers or appointed to serve as the monarch's Privy Council.

Following the magistrates came the young and highly

distinguished minister, who was expected to deliver the religious sermon for the anniversary. During that time period, the ministry was the profession where intellectual talent showed itself much more than in politics; for—setting aside any higher calling—it provided incentives strong enough, through the nearly worshipful reverence of the community, to attract the most ambitious individuals to its ranks. Even political power—as demonstrated by Increase Mather—was within reach of a successful clergyman.

Those who watched him now observed that never since Mr. Dimmesdale first stepped onto New England's shores had he displayed such vigor as was evident in his stride and bearing as he maintained his pace in the procession. There was none of the weakness in his step that marked other occasions; his body wasn't hunched over; nor did his hand rest ominously upon his chest. Yet, if one looked at the minister carefully, his strength appeared to come from something other than his physical body. It could have been spiritual, given to him through divine intervention. It might have been the excitement that comes from that powerful stimulant which is created only in the intense heat of serious and prolonged thinking. Or perhaps his delicate nature was energized by the loud and sharp music that rose toward heaven and lifted him up on its rising current. Still, his expression was so distant that one might wonder whether Mr. Dimmesdale even noticed the music. His body was there, moving forward with unusual strength. But where was his consciousness? It was far away and deep within its own realm, working with supernatural intensity to organize a parade of dignified thoughts that would soon emerge from there; and so he saw nothing, heard nothing, knew nothing of his surroundings; but the spiritual force lifted up his weak body and carried it along, unaware of its weight, and transformed it into spirit like itself. People of exceptional intelligence who have become obsessed possess this occasional ability for tremendous effort, into which they pour the energy of many days, and then remain drained for just as many more.

Hester Prynne stared intently at the minister and felt a gloomy feeling wash over her, though she couldn't understand why or where it came from, except that he seemed so far removed from her world and completely out of her reach. She had expected that at least one look of recognition would pass between them. She remembered the shadowy forest with its small clearing of isolation, love, and pain, and the moss-covered fallen tree where they had sat holding hands, mixing their sorrowful and passionate conversation with the sad babbling of the stream. How intimately they had known each other back then! Could this really be the same man? She barely recognized him now! There he was, walking proudly past, surrounded by the magnificent music and the procession of distinguished and respected church leaders; he was so unreachable in his social position, and even more so in that distant realm of his unsympathetic thoughts through which she now saw him! Her heart sank at the thought that everything must have been an illusion, and that no matter how vividly she had experienced it, there could be no real connection between the minister and herself. There was enough of the feminine nature in Hester that she could hardly forgive him—especially not now, when the heavy footsteps of their approaching destiny could be heard coming closer and closer and closer!—for being able to so completely remove himself from the world they had shared, while she fumbled in the darkness, reaching out with her cold hands, unable to find him.

Pearl either noticed and reacted to her mother's emotions, or she herself sensed the distance and unreachable quality that had surrounded the minister. As the procession moved past, the child grew restless, moving back and forth like a bird about to take flight. After everyone had passed by, she looked up into Hester's face.

"Mother," she said, "was that the same minister who kissed me by the brook?"

"Be quiet, dear little Pearl!" her mother whispered. "We can't always talk in public about what happens to us in private."

"I couldn't be certain it was really him; he looked so different," the child went on. "Otherwise I would have run straight to him and asked him to kiss me right there in front of everyone, just like he did back there among those dark old trees. What do you think the minister would have said, mother? Would he have pressed his hand against his chest, glared at me, and told me to go away?"

"What should he say, Pearl," Hester replied, "except that it wasn't the right time to kiss, and that kisses shouldn't be given in the marketplace? It's a good thing for you, foolish child, that you didn't speak to him!"

Another variation of the same feeling regarding Mr. Dimmesdale came from someone whose peculiar behavior—or madness, as we would call it—drove her to do something few townspeople would have dared: she started a conversation with the woman wearing the scarlet letter, right there in public. This was Mistress Hibbins, who had dressed herself magnificently in a triple ruff, an embroidered stomacher, a gown made of rich velvet, and carried a gold-headed cane as she came out to watch the procession. This elderly woman had gained a reputation (which later cost her nothing less than her life) for being a key participant in all the witchcraft activities that were constantly taking place, so the crowd parted before her and seemed afraid to let her clothing touch them, as if it carried disease within its splendid folds. When people saw her standing with Hester Prynne—despite the kindness many now felt toward Hester—the fear that Mistress Hibbins inspired doubled, causing everyone to move away from that section of the marketplace where the two women stood.

"Can you imagine such a thing!" the old woman whispered secretly to Hester. "Look at that holy man over there! The people consider him a saint walking among us, and I have to admit he certainly appears to be one! Who would ever think, seeing him march in that procession, that just a short time ago he left his study—probably still pondering some Hebrew scripture passage—to take a walk in the woods! Oh yes! We understand what that really means, Hester Prynne! But honestly, I'm finding it difficult to believe he's the same person. I've seen many church members walking behind that music who have danced to the same rhythm as me, when the Devil himself was playing the fiddle, and perhaps even an Indian medicine man or a wizard from Lapland joined hands with us! That's nothing unusual when a woman understands how the world works. But this minister! Could you say for certain, Hester, whether he was the same man who met you on that forest path?"

"Ma'am, I don't know what you're talking about," Hester Prynne replied, sensing that Mistress Hibbins was mentally unstable; yet she felt strangely alarmed and filled with dread by the certainty with which the woman claimed a personal relationship existed between so many people (including herself) and the Devil. "It's not my place to speak carelessly about a scholarly and devout minister of God's Word, like the Reverend Mr. Dimmesdale!"

"Shame on you, woman, shame!" cried the old lady, shaking her finger at Hester. "Do you think I have been to the forest so many times, and still have no skill to judge who else has been there? Yes; even though no leaf of the wild garlands, which they wore while they danced, remains in their hair! I know you, Hester; for I see the token. We may all see it in the sunshine; and it glows like a red flame in the dark. You wear it openly; so there need be no question about that. But this minister! Let me tell you, in your ear! When the Black Man sees one of his own servants, signed and sealed, so shy of owning to the bond as is the Reverend Mr. Dimmesdale, he has a way of arranging matters so that the mark shall be revealed in open daylight to the eyes of all the world! What is it that the minister seeks to hide, with his hand always over his heart? Ha, Hester Prynne!"

"What is it, good Mistress Hibbins?" little Pearl asked eagerly. "Have you seen it?"

"It doesn't matter, darling!" replied Mistress Hibbins, giving Pearl a deep bow. "You'll see it yourself, sooner or later. They say, child, that you come from the bloodline of the Prince of the Air! Will you ride with me some beautiful night to see your father? Then you'll understand why the minister keeps his hand over his heart!"

Laughing so sharply that everyone in the marketplace could hear her, the strange old woman left.

By this time, the opening prayer had been given in the meeting house, and the voice of Reverend Mr. Dimmesdale could be heard beginning his sermon. An overwhelming urge kept Hester close to that place. Since the sacred building was too crowded to allow another listener inside, she positioned herself right next to the pillory scaffold. She was close enough to hear the entire sermon, though it reached her ears as an unclear but changing murmur and rhythm of the minister's very distinctive voice.

This voice was itself a magnificent gift; so much so that a listener who understood nothing of the language the preacher spoke could still be moved back and forth by the sound and rhythm alone. Like all music, it expressed passion and deep feeling, conveying both powerful and gentle emotions in a language that speaks naturally to the human heart, no matter where someone was raised. Though the sound was muffled as it traveled through the church walls, Hester Prynne listened so intently and felt such a deep connection that the sermon held meaning for her completely separate from the words she couldn't make out. These words, if heard more clearly, might have actually been a cruder way to communicate and could have blocked the spiritual understanding. Sometimes she caught the quiet undertone, like wind settling down to rest; then she rose with it as it climbed through increasing levels of beauty and strength, until its fullness seemed to surround her with a feeling of wonder and serious majesty. Yet even when the voice became most impressive, it always carried an essential quality of sadness. Whether loud or soft, it expressed suffering—the whisper or cry, as one might imagine, of humanity in pain, touching something sensitive in every heart! At times this deep current of sorrow was all that could be heard, and barely heard at that, sighing through an empty silence. But even when the minister's voice became loud and commanding—when it poured out uncontrollably upward—when it reached its greatest width and power, filling the church so completely that it seemed to break through the solid walls and spread into the open air—still, if someone listened carefully and with purpose, they could detect that same cry of pain. What was it? The complaint of a human heart, heavy with sorrow, perhaps guilty, sharing its secret—whether of guilt or grief—with the great heart of humanity; asking for understanding or forgiveness—at every moment—in each tone—and never without response! It was this deep and constant undertone that gave the minister his most fitting power.

During this entire time, Hester remained motionless like a statue at the base of the scaffold. Even if the minister's voice hadn't held her there, she would have felt an irresistible pull to that place where her life of shame had begun. She experienced a feeling—too vague to form into a clear thought, yet pressing heavily on her mind—that her entire existence, both past and future, was tied to this location, as if it were the single point that brought meaning to her whole life.

Little Pearl had left her mother's side and was playing freely throughout the marketplace. Her unpredictable and sparkling presence brought joy to the somber crowd, much like a brightly colored bird lights up an entire tree of dark leaves by darting back and forth, partially visible and partially hidden among the shadowy branches. Her movements were flowing but often sharp and erratic. This reflected the restless energy of her spirit, which today was twice as tireless in its dancing motion because it responded to and trembled with her mother's anxiety. Whenever Pearl noticed something that caught her constantly active and roaming curiosity, she rushed toward it and, as one might say, claimed that person or object as her own possession, at least as much as she wanted it, but without giving up even the smallest amount of control over her own actions in return. The Puritans watched, and even when they smiled, they were still inclined to call the child a devil's offspring because of the mysterious combination of beauty and strangeness that radiated from her small form and sparkled through her movements. She ran up and stared directly at the wild Indian, and he became aware of a nature more untamed than his own. Then, with natural boldness but still maintaining her characteristic distance, she darted into the middle of a group of sailors, those dark-skinned wild men of the sea, just as the Indians were wild men of the land, and they stared at Pearl with wonder and admiration, as if a piece of sea foam had taken the form of a little girl and been given a soul made of sea-fire, the kind that flashes beneath a ship's bow during the night.

One of these sailors—the ship captain who had spoken to Hester Prynne—was so captivated by Pearl's appearance that he tried to grab her, intending to steal a kiss. Finding it as impossible to touch her as it would be to catch a hummingbird in mid-flight, he removed the gold chain that was wrapped around his hat and tossed it to the child. Pearl immediately wound it around her neck and waist with such joyful grace that, once it was there, it seemed to become part of her, and it was hard to picture her without it.

"Your mother is that woman over there with the scarlet letter," said the sailor. "Will you take her a message from me?"

"If the message pleases me, I will," Pearl replied.

"Then tell her," he replied, "that I spoke again with the dark-faced, hump-shouldered old doctor, and he promises to bring his friend, the gentleman she knows of, aboard with him. So let your mother worry about nothing except herself and you. Will you tell her this, you little witch?"

"Mistress Hibbins says my father is the Prince of the Air!" cried Pearl, with a mischievous smile. "If you call me that awful name, I'll tell him about you; and he will chase your ship with a storm!"

Following a winding path across the marketplace, the child made her way back to her mother and shared what the sailor had told her. Hester's powerful, composed, and steadily resilient spirit nearly collapsed at that moment, seeing this dark and forbidding face of unavoidable fate, which—just when an escape route appeared to open for the minister and herself from their maze of suffering—revealed itself with a merciless smile directly blocking their way forward.

With her mind troubled by the terrible confusion that the ship captain's news had caused her, she also faced another ordeal. Many people were present from the surrounding countryside who had frequently heard about the scarlet letter, and to whom it had become frightening through countless false or exaggerated stories, but who had never seen it with their own eyes. These people, after running out of other forms of entertainment, now crowded around Hester Prynne with crude and rude pushiness. Shameless as this behavior was, however, it could not bring them closer than several yards away. At that distance they remained standing, held there by the repelling force of the disgust that the mysterious symbol created. The entire group of sailors, similarly, noticing the crowd of onlookers and learning the meaning of the scarlet letter, came and pushed their sun-weathered and dangerous-looking faces into the circle. Even the Indians were influenced by a kind of cold reflection of the white man's curiosity, and, moving silently through the crowd, fixed their snake-like black eyes on Hester's chest, thinking perhaps that the person wearing this brilliantly embroidered symbol must be someone of great importance among her people. Finally the residents of the town, their own interest in this old matter slowly awakening again through sympathy with what they saw others feeling, wandered lazily to the same area and tormented Hester Prynne, perhaps more than all the others, with their calm, familiar stare at her well-known shame. Hester saw and recognized the same faces of that group of women who had waited for her to emerge from the prison door seven years ago, all except one, the youngest and only kind one among them, whose burial dress she had since sewn. At this final moment, when she was so soon to throw away the burning letter, it had strangely become the center of more attention and excitement, and was thus made to burn her chest more painfully than at any time since the first day she wore it.

While Hester stood in that magical circle of shame, where the clever cruelty of her punishment seemed to have trapped her forever, the remarkable preacher was looking down from the holy pulpit at an audience whose deepest souls had surrendered to his influence. The revered minister in the church! The woman with the scarlet letter in the marketplace! What mind would have been bold enough to imagine that the same burning mark of disgrace was on both of them!

Chapter 23: The Revelation of The Scarlet Letter.

The powerful voice that had lifted the souls of the listening congregation like rising ocean waves finally fell silent. A deep quiet followed, as profound as the silence that should come after hearing divine prophecies. Then came a murmur and subdued commotion, as if the listeners, freed from the powerful enchantment that had carried them into the speaker's mind, were coming back to themselves, still weighed down by their reverence and amazement. Moments later, the crowd began streaming out through the church doors. Now that it was over, they needed different air, better suited to sustain the crude and worldly existence they were returning to, rather than the atmosphere the preacher had transformed into fiery words and filled with the rich essence of his thoughts.

Once they stepped outside, their excitement burst into conversation. The street and marketplace buzzed from one end to the other with praise for the minister. His listeners couldn't settle down until they had shared with each other what everyone already knew better than they could express or comprehend. Based on their collective account, no man had ever spoken with such wisdom, such elevated thought, and such sacred spirit as he had that day; nor had divine inspiration ever flowed through human lips more clearly than it had through his. Its power could be witnessed, as if it were, coming down upon him, taking hold of him, and constantly lifting him beyond the written sermon that lay in front of him, filling him with thoughts that must have amazed him as much as they did his congregation. His topic, it seemed, had been the relationship between God and human communities, with particular attention to the New England they were establishing in this untamed land. And as he approached the conclusion, a prophetic spirit had descended upon him, compelling him toward its purpose as powerfully as the ancient prophets of Israel had been compelled; except that while the Jewish visionaries had proclaimed judgment and destruction for their nation, his calling was to predict a noble and magnificent future for this newly assembled people of the Lord. Yet throughout everything, and through the entire sermon, there had been a persistent deep, melancholy undercurrent of sorrow, which could only be understood as the natural grief of someone about to depart this world. Yes; their beloved minister—who loved them all so deeply that he couldn't ascend to heaven without a heavy heart—carried the sense of approaching death, and would soon leave them mourning! This notion of his brief time remaining on earth provided the final touch to the impact the preacher had created; it was as though an angel, on his journey to the heavens, had spread his luminous wings over the people for a moment—both shadow and brilliance at once—and had poured down a cascade of divine truths upon them.

Thus, there had come to the Reverend Mr. Dimmesdale—as happens to most people in their different walks of life, though they rarely realize it until they look back from a distance—a period in his life more brilliant and triumphant than any before it, or any that could come after. At this moment, he stood at the very highest peak of superiority that a clergyman could reach in early New England, elevated by his intellectual gifts, vast learning, powerful speaking ability, and a reputation for pure holiness, especially during those days when the ministerial profession itself provided a noble platform. This was the position the minister held as he bowed his head forward on the pulpit cushions at the end of his Election Sermon. Meanwhile, Hester Prynne stood beside the pillory scaffold, with the scarlet letter still blazing on her chest!

The sound of music rang out once more, accompanied by the rhythmic marching of the military escort as they emerged from the church door. The procession would form up there and proceed to the town hall, where a formal banquet would bring the day's ceremonies to a close.

Once again, the procession of respected and dignified leaders could be seen moving through a wide path among the people, who stepped back respectfully on both sides as the Governor and magistrates, the elderly and wise men, the sacred ministers, and all who were distinguished and celebrated, walked forward into their midst. When they had fully entered the marketplace, their arrival was welcomed by a loud cheer. This cheer—though it certainly may have gained extra strength and intensity from the childlike devotion that the era showed to its leaders—was understood to be an unstoppable burst of excitement sparked in the listeners by that elevated style of speaking which was still echoing in their ears. Each person felt the urge within himself, and at the same moment, picked it up from his neighbor. Inside the church, it had barely been contained; under the open sky, it rang upward to the highest point. There were enough human beings present, and enough deeply stirred and harmonious emotion, to create that more powerful sound than the musical tones of the wind, or the thunder, or the crash of the ocean; indeed that tremendous rise of many voices, merged into one great voice by the shared impulse which also creates one enormous heart from the many. Never from the land of New England had such a cheer risen up! Never on New England soil had there stood a man so respected by his fellow mortals as this preacher!

How was he doing then? Weren't there shining fragments of a halo floating in the air around his head? With his spirit so refined and elevated to such divine status by his devoted followers, did his feet actually touch the ground as he walked in the procession?

As the rows of soldiers and civic leaders continued forward, everyone's gaze turned toward the spot where they could see the minister approaching among them. The shouting faded to a whisper as one section of the crowd after another caught sight of him. How weak and pale he appeared, despite all his success! The strength—or rather, the divine inspiration that had sustained him until he could deliver the holy message that carried its own power from heaven—had left him now that it had so faithfully completed its purpose. The radiance that they had just witnessed glowing on his face was gone, like a flame that dies down helplessly among the dying coals. With such a deathly pallor, it barely seemed like the face of a living man; with life so faint within him, he could hardly be called a man as he stumbled along his path so weakly, yet stumbled without falling!

One of his fellow clergymen—the respected John Wilson—noticed the condition Mr. Dimmesdale was in after the departing surge of mental and emotional energy had left him, and quickly stepped forward to provide assistance. The minister shakily but firmly pushed away the old man's outstretched arm. He continued walking forward, though this movement could hardly be called walking, as it more closely resembled the unsteady attempts of a baby reaching toward its mother's open arms that beckoned it onward. Now, though his final steps were barely noticeable, he had arrived directly across from the familiar, weather-stained scaffold where, so long ago, with all those bleak years stretching between then and now, Hester Prynne had faced the world's shameful gaze. There stood Hester, gripping little Pearl's hand! And there was the scarlet letter displayed on her chest! The minister stopped here, even though the music continued playing the grand and celebratory march that guided the procession forward. The music called to him—onward to the celebration!—but here he stopped.

Bellingham had been watching him anxiously for the past few moments. He now stepped out of his position in the procession and moved forward to offer help, sensing from Mr. Dimmesdale's appearance that the man would surely collapse otherwise. However, something in Dimmesdale's expression made the magistrate step back, even though he wasn't someone who typically heeded the subtle signals that pass between souls. The crowd, in the meantime, watched with reverence and amazement. In their eyes, this physical weakness was simply another manifestation of the minister's divine power; it wouldn't have seemed like too great a miracle for someone so sacred to rise up before their very eyes, growing fainter and brighter, and finally disappearing into heaven's light.

He turned toward the scaffold and stretched out his arms.

"Hester," he said, "come here! Come, my little Pearl!"

He looked at them with a horrifying expression, yet there was something both gentle and strangely victorious in his gaze. The child, with the bird-like movement that was one of her traits, rushed to him and wrapped her arms around his knees. Hester Prynne—slowly, as if driven by unavoidable destiny and against her deepest desire—also moved closer, but stopped before reaching him. At that moment, old Roger Chillingworth pushed himself through the crowd—or perhaps, so dark, troubled, and wicked was his appearance, he emerged from some underground realm—to pull back his victim from what he intended to do! Whatever the case, the old man lunged forward and grabbed the minister by the arm.

"You're insane, stop! What are you trying to do?" he whispered urgently. "Send that woman away! Get rid of this child! Everything will be fine! Don't destroy your reputation and die in disgrace! I can still save you! Do you want to bring shame upon your holy calling?"

"Ha, tempter! I think you are too late!" answered the minister, meeting his gaze fearfully but firmly. "Your power is not what it once was! With God's help, I shall escape you now!"

He once again reached out his hand to the woman who wore the scarlet letter.

"Hester Prynne," he cried out with intense urgency, "in the name of Him who is both terrible and merciful, who grants me the grace at this final moment to do what I prevented myself from doing seven years ago because of my own grievous sin and wretched suffering—come here now and wrap your strength around me! Your strength, Hester, but let it be guided by the will that God has given me! This miserable and wronged old man is fighting against it with everything he has—with all his own power and the devil's too! Come, Hester, come! Help me up to that scaffold!"

The crowd was in chaos. The distinguished and respected men

who stood closest to the clergyman were so caught off guard and so confused about the meaning of what they witnessed—unable to accept the explanation that seemed most obvious, or to think of any other—that they stayed silent and motionless as observers of the divine judgment that appeared to be unfolding. They watched the minister, leaning against Hester's shoulder and supported by her arm around him, walk toward the scaffold and climb its steps; meanwhile, the small hand of the child born from sin remained clasped in his. Old Roger Chillingworth followed behind, as someone deeply involved in this drama of guilt and suffering in which they had all played parts, and therefore fully deserving to witness its final scene.

"If you had searched the entire world," he said, looking darkly at the clergyman, "there was no place so hidden—no high place or low place where you could have escaped me—except on this very scaffold!"

"Thank God for leading me here!" the minister replied.

Yet he trembled and turned to Hester with doubt and anxiety clearly visible in his eyes, made even more obvious by the weak smile that played across his lips.

"Isn't this better," he murmured, "than what we dreamed of in the forest?"

"I don't know! I don't know!" she quickly answered. "Better? Yes; so we might all die, and little Pearl die along with us!"

"For you and Pearl, let it be as God decides," said the minister; "and God is merciful! Let me now do what he has made clear before my eyes. For, Hester, I am a dying man. So let me hurry to take my shame upon myself!"

Partially supported by Hester Prynne and grasping little Pearl's hand, Reverend Mr. Dimmesdale faced the distinguished and respected leaders, the sacred ministers who were his fellow clergymen, and the people whose compassionate hearts were deeply shocked yet filled with sympathetic tears, understanding that some profound matter of life—one that, though steeped in sin, was equally filled with suffering and remorse—was about to be revealed to them. The sun, having barely passed noon, cast its light upon the minister and clearly outlined his form as he stood apart from all others on earth to enter his plea of guilt before the tribunal of Divine Justice.

"People of New England!" he cried out, his voice rising above them all, high and solemn and majestic—yet it always carried a tremor, and sometimes a shriek that seemed to emerge from an endless depth of remorse and suffering—"you who have loved me! You who have considered me holy! Look at me here, the greatest sinner in the world! Finally! At last! I stand on the very spot where I should have stood seven years ago; here, with this woman, whose arm supports me more than my own feeble strength that brought me here, keeping me from collapsing face-down on the ground at this terrible moment! Look at the scarlet letter that Hester wears! All of you have shuddered at the sight of it! Wherever she has walked—wherever she may have hoped to find peace in her miserable burden—it has cast a sinister glow of fear and horrible disgust all around her. But there stood someone among you whose mark of sin and shame has never made you shudder!"

At this moment, it appeared that the minister would have to leave the rest of his secret unspoken. However, he battled against his physical weakness and, even more so, the weakness of spirit that was trying to overcome him. He rejected all help and stepped forward with intense emotion, moving one step ahead of the woman and the child.

"It was on him!" he went on, speaking with fierce intensity, completely determined to reveal everything. "God saw it! The angels constantly pointed at it! The Devil knew it well and tormented it endlessly with his burning touch! But he cleverly concealed it from people and moved among you appearing like a spirit—sorrowful because he seemed so pure in this sinful world, and melancholy because he longed for his heavenly family! Now, in his final moments, he stands before you! He asks you to look once more at Hester's scarlet letter! He's telling you that despite all its mysterious terror, it's merely a shadow of what he carries on his own chest, and even his own red mark of shame is nothing more than a symbol of what has burned into his deepest soul! Does anyone here doubt God's judgment upon a sinner? Look! See the terrible proof of it!"

Shall we not meet again?

With a sudden, jerking movement, he ripped the ministerial band away from his chest. It was revealed! But it would be disrespectful to describe what was shown. For a moment, the eyes of the horrified crowd focused on the terrible sight; while the minister stood there, his face glowing with triumph, like someone who had achieved victory in a moment of intense suffering. Then he collapsed onto the scaffold! Hester partially lifted him and held his head against her chest. Old Roger Chillingworth knelt down next to him, his face empty and lifeless, as if all vitality had drained from it.

"You have escaped me!" he repeated more than once. "You have escaped me!"

"May God forgive you!" said the minister. "You, too, have deeply sinned!"

He pulled his fading gaze away from the elderly man and focused it on the woman and the child.

"My little Pearl," he said weakly, and there was a sweet and gentle smile across his face, like a spirit settling into deep rest; in fact, now that the burden had been lifted, it seemed almost as if he wanted to play with the child. "Dear little Pearl, will you kiss me now? You wouldn't back there in the forest! But now you will?"

Pearl kissed his lips. A spell was broken. The powerful scene of sorrow, in which the untamed child had played a role, had awakened all her compassion; and as her tears dropped onto her father's cheek, they promised that she would mature surrounded by human happiness and sadness, and would not eternally fight against the world, but would become a woman within it. Toward her mother as well, Pearl's mission as a bearer of pain was completely accomplished.

"Hester," said the clergyman, "farewell!"

"Won't we see each other again?" she whispered, leaning her face close to his. "Won't we spend our eternal life together? Certainly, we must have saved each other through all this suffering! You're looking far into eternity with those bright, dying eyes! So tell me what you see?"

"Quiet, Hester, quiet!" he said, his voice shaking with deep seriousness. "The law we broke!—the sin so terribly exposed here!—let only these fill your thoughts! I'm afraid! I'm afraid! It may be that when we forgot our God—when we violated our respect for each other's soul—it became pointless from that moment to hope we could meet again in an eternal and pure reunion. God knows; and He is merciful! He has shown his mercy most of all through my suffering. By giving me this burning agony to carry on my chest! By sending that dark and terrible old man to keep the torture always blazing hot! By bringing me here to die this death of victorious shame before the people! If any of these torments had been missing, I would have been lost forever! Praise be to his name! His will be done! Farewell!"

The minister spoke that last word as he drew his final breath. The crowd, which had remained silent until that moment, suddenly erupted in a strange, profound sound of reverence and amazement—a sound that couldn't yet form into actual words, but instead emerged as a deep murmur that seemed to follow heavily in the wake of his departing soul.

Chapter 24: Conclusion

After many days, when enough time had passed for people to organize their thoughts about the previous scene, there was more than one version of what had been witnessed on the scaffold.

Most of the witnesses claimed they saw a SCARLET LETTER on the unfortunate minister's chest—looking exactly like the one Hester Prynne wore—burned into his flesh. When it came to how it got there, people offered different explanations, though all of them were just guesswork. Some insisted that Reverend Dimmesdale had started punishing himself on the very same day Hester Prynne first put on her shameful mark—a self-inflicted torture that he continued through many unsuccessful attempts at penance. Others argued that the mark didn't appear until much later, when old Roger Chillingworth, being a powerful sorcerer, made it show up through magic and deadly poisons. Still others—those who best understood the minister's sensitive nature and how powerfully his mind affected his body—whispered their belief that this terrible symbol came from guilt constantly eating away at him, gnawing from deep inside his heart outward, until it finally revealed God's awful judgment through the visible appearance of the letter. Readers can decide which of these theories to believe. We've shared all the information we could gather about this mysterious sign, and now that it has served its purpose, we would gladly erase its deep impression from our own minds, where long thinking about it has made it disturbingly clear.

It is strange, however, that certain people who witnessed the entire scene and claimed they never once looked away from Reverend Mr. Dimmesdale insisted there was no mark whatsoever on his chest, no more than would be found on a newborn baby's. Furthermore, according to their account, his final words neither acknowledged nor even hinted at any connection between himself and the sin for which Hester Prynne had worn the scarlet letter for so long. According to these highly respected witnesses, the minister, aware that he was dying and conscious that the crowd's reverence had already placed him among saints and angels, had chosen to die in the arms of that fallen woman to show the world how completely worthless even the best of human righteousness truly is. After spending his life working for humanity's spiritual benefit, he had turned his death into a parable to teach his followers the powerful and sorrowful truth that in the eyes of Infinite Purity, we are all equally sinners. His purpose was to show them that even the holiest person among us has only risen high enough above others to see more clearly the Mercy that looks down from above, and to reject more completely the illusion of human worthiness that tries to reach upward. Without questioning such an important truth, we must be permitted to view this interpretation of Mr. Dimmesdale's story as simply an example of the stubborn loyalty with which a person's friends—especially those of a clergyman—will sometimes defend his reputation, even when evidence as clear as midday sunlight on the scarlet letter proves him to be a false and sin-stained mortal.

The main source we have relied on—an old manuscript compiled from spoken accounts of people, some of whom had personally known Hester Prynne, while others had heard the story from witnesses of that time—completely supports the perspective presented in the previous pages. Among the many lessons that emerge from the poor minister's wretched experience, we express only this one in words: "Be true! Be true! Be true! Show openly to the world, if not your worst qualities, then at least some characteristic from which the worst might be understood!"

Nothing was more striking than the transformation that occurred, almost instantly after Mr. Dimmesdale's death, in the appearance and behavior of the elderly man known as Roger Chillingworth. All his strength and energy—all his life force and mental power—seemed to abandon him at once; so much so that he literally withered away, shrank up, and nearly disappeared from human view, like a plant torn from its roots that lies dying in the sunlight. This miserable man had built his entire existence around pursuing and methodically carrying out revenge; and when, through its complete victory and fulfillment, that wicked driving force was left without any further purpose to sustain it, when, in essence, there was no more evil work left on earth for him to accomplish, all that remained was for this dehumanized soul to go where his Master would provide him with plenty of tasks and pay him his due wages. But toward all these ghostly figures who have been our close companions for so long—Roger Chillingworth as well as his associates—we would prefer to show compassion. It presents a fascinating topic for observation and investigation, whether hatred and love might not be fundamentally the same emotion. Each, when fully developed, requires a deep level of closeness and understanding of the heart; each makes one person dependent on another for nourishment of their emotions and spiritual existence; each leaves the intense lover, or the equally intense hater, abandoned and alone when the object of their passion is taken away. From a philosophical perspective, therefore, these two emotions appear to be essentially identical, except that one is viewed in heavenly light, while the other appears in a dark and ominous glow. In the realm of the spirit, the old doctor and the minister—who have been each other's victims—may, without realizing it, have discovered their earthly supply of hatred and hostility transformed into pure love.

Setting aside this discussion, we need to share some business matters with the reader. When old Roger Chillingworth died, which happened within the year, his last will and testament left a very substantial amount of property to little Pearl, Hester Prynne's daughter. This property was located both here and in England, and Governor Bellingham and the Reverend Mr. Wilson served as executors of the will.

So Pearl—the elf-child, the demon offspring, as some people up to that time continued to consider her—became the wealthiest heiress of her era in the New World. Most likely, this situation brought about a significant change in public opinion; and if the mother and child had stayed here, little Pearl, when she reached marriageable age, might have mixed her untamed blood with the family line of the most devoted Puritan among them all. However, not long after the physician's death, the woman who wore the scarlet letter vanished, and Pearl disappeared with her. For many years, although a unclear report would occasionally make its way across the ocean—like a formless piece of driftwood washed ashore with the letters of a name carved on it—no news of them that was definitely reliable was ever received. The story of the scarlet letter became a legend. Its power, though, remained strong, and kept the scaffold frightening where the poor minister had died, and also the cottage by the seashore where Hester Prynne had lived. Near this last location, one afternoon, some children were playing when they saw a tall woman in a gray robe approaching the cottage door. Throughout all those years it had never been opened even once; but either she unlocked it, or the rotting wood and iron gave way to her touch, or she slipped through these obstacles like a shadow—and in any case, she went inside.

At the doorway she stopped and turned partway around, perhaps because the thought of entering alone, so completely transformed, into the home where she had once lived such an intense life, felt more bleak and lonely than even she could endure. But her pause lasted only a moment, though it was long enough to reveal a scarlet letter on her chest.

Hester's Return

And Hester Prynne had returned, and taken up her long-abandoned shame! But where was little Pearl? If she was still alive, she would now be in the prime and beauty of early womanhood.

No one knew—nor ever found out with complete certainty—whether the fairy-like child had died so young in an unmarried woman's grave; or whether her wild, passionate nature had been gentled and tamed, and made capable of a woman's tender happiness. But throughout the rest of Hester's life, there were signs that the hermit of the scarlet letter was loved and cared for by someone living in another country. Letters arrived with coat-of-arms seals on them, though the designs were unknown to English heraldry. In the cottage there were items of comfort and luxury that Hester never bothered to use, but which only wealth could have bought, and affection could have thought to give her. There were small things too, little decorations, beautiful gifts showing constant remembrance, that must have been made by skilled fingers, driven by a loving heart. And once, Hester was seen embroidering a baby's outfit with such extravagant richness of golden decoration that it would have caused a public uproar if any infant dressed in such clothing had been shown to our plainly-dressed community.

In the end, the townspeople of that time believed—and Mr. Surveyor Pue, who conducted his research a century afterward, believed—and one of his recent successors in office, furthermore, firmly believes—that Pearl was not only still living, but had married, found happiness, and remembered her mother fondly, and that she would have welcomed that sorrowful and solitary mother into her home with great joy.

But there was a more genuine life for Hester Prynne here, in New England, than in that distant place where Pearl had made her home. This was where her sin had occurred; this was where her grief had unfolded; and this was where her repentance still needed to happen. She had come back, therefore, and taken up again—by her own choice, since not even the harshest judge of that strict era would have forced it upon her—taken up again the symbol about which we have told such a dark story. It never left her chest again.

However, as the difficult, contemplative, and selfless years that formed Hester's life passed by, the scarlet letter stopped being a mark of shame that drew the world's contempt and cruelty, and instead became a symbol of something to feel sorry about, and to view with wonder, yet with respect as well. And, since Hester Prynne had no selfish goals, nor lived in any way for her own gain and pleasure, people brought all their troubles and confusion to her, and asked for her advice, seeing her as someone who had herself endured great suffering. Women, particularly—dealing with the constant struggles of hurt, exhausted, betrayed, misunderstood, or mistaken and sinful love—or carrying the heavy weight of a heart that remained closed because it was neither valued nor wanted—came to Hester's cottage, asking why they felt so miserable, and what could help them! Hester comforted and advised them as well as she could. She also told them of her strong conviction that, at some happier time, when the world would be ready for it, in God's perfect timing, a new truth would be revealed, meant to build the entire relationship between man and woman on a more solid foundation of shared joy. Earlier in her life, Hester had foolishly thought that she herself might be the chosen messenger, but had long ago understood the impossibility that any mission involving divine and mysterious truth could be entrusted to a woman marked by sin, weighed down by disgrace, or even carrying the burden of lifelong sadness. The messenger and teacher of the coming revelation must indeed be a woman, but one who is noble, innocent, and beautiful; and wise, furthermore, not through dark suffering, but through the heavenly experience of happiness; and demonstrating how holy love should bring us joy, by the most reliable proof of a life lived successfully toward that goal!

So said Hester Prynne, and she looked down sadly at the scarlet letter. And after many, many years, a new grave was dug near an old and sunken one in that burial ground beside which

King's Chapel was later built. The new grave was close to that old and sunken grave, yet with space between them, as if the dust of the two who slept there had no right to mix together. Yet one tombstone served for both graves. All around were monuments carved with family coats of arms; and on this simple slate slab—as the curious investigator may still see today, and puzzle over its meaning—there appeared what looked like an engraved coat of arms. It bore a design, whose heraldic description might serve as a motto and brief summary of our now finished story; so dark it is, and brightened only by one eternally glowing point of light that is gloomier than the shadow itself:—

"On a field, sable, the letter A, gules."

THE END

Thank You For Reading

You've Just Read a Piece of the Greatest Library Ever Rebuilt

Thank you for reading.

This book is one of thousands we're restoring, reimagining, and translating as part of the **Modern Library of Alexandria** — a global movement to preserve and share humanity's most important ideas.

What was once lost to fire and time is now rising again — not just as memory, but as living, breathing knowledge, freely accessible to all.

What You Can Do Next:

- **Keep Reading.**

  Discover more legendary works — in beautiful print, audiobook, or digital form — at LibraryofAlexandria.com.

- **Build Your Own Library.**

  Every title is available as a paperback, hardcover, or collectible boxset — at true printing cost. Craft a personal library worthy of display.

- **Spread the Light.**

  Share this book. Tell others about the movement. Help us translate every timeless work into every language, so no reader is ever left behind.

By finishing this book, you've already taken part in something extraordinary.

Join us at LibraryofAlexandria.com

Together, we're rebuilding the greatest library the world has ever known.

With appreciation,

The Modern Library of Alexandria Team

Visit:
www.libraryofalexandria.com
Or scan the code below:

www.ingramcontent.com/pod-product-compliance
Lightning Source LLC
Chambersburg PA
CBHW011354010726
47494CB00008B/2313